A Vietnamese Kitchen

Treasured Family Recipes

THE HIPPOCRENE COOKBOOK LIBRARY

Afghan Food & Cookery
African Cooking, Best of Regional
Albanian Cooking, Best of
Alps, Cuisines of The
Aprovecho: A Mexican-American Border Cookbook
Argentina Cooks!, Exp. Ed.
Austrian Cuisine, Best of, Exp. Ed.
Bolivian Kitchen, My Mother's
Brazilian Cookery, The Art of
Bulgarian Cooking, Traditional
Burma, Flavors of
Cajun Women, Cooking with
Calabria, Cucina di
Caucasus Mountains, Cuisines of the
Chile, Tasting
Colombian Cooking, Secrets of
Croatian Cooking, Best of, Exp. Ed.
Czech Cooking, Best of, Exp. Ed.
Danube, All Along The, Exp. Ed.
Dutch Cooking, Art of, Exp. Ed.
Egyptian Cooking
Filipino Food, Fine
Finnish Cooking, Best of
French Caribbean Cuisine
French Fashion, Cooking in the (Bilingual)
Germany, Spoonfuls of
Greek Cuisine, The Best of, Exp. Ed.
Gypsy Feast
Haiti, Taste of, Exp. Ed.
Havana Cookbook, Old (Bilingual)
Hungarian Cookbook
Hungarian Cooking, Art of, Rev. Ed.
Icelandic Food & Cookery
India, Flavorful (Gujarati)
Indian Spice Kitchen
International Dictionary of Gastronomy
Irish-Style, Feasting Galore
Italian Cuisine, Treasury of (Bilingual)
Japanese Home Cooking
Korean Cuisine, Best of
Laotian Cooking, Simple
Latvia, Taste of

Lithuanian Cooking, Art of
Macau, Taste of
Middle Eastern Kitchen, The
Mongolian Cooking, Imperial
New Hampshire: from Farm to Kitchen
New Jersey Cookbook, Farms and Foods of the Garden State:
Norway, Tastes and Tales of
Persian Cooking, Art of
Pied Noir Cookbook: French Sephardic Cuisine from Algeria
Poland's Gourmet Cuisine
Polish Cooking, Best of, Exp. Ed.
Polish Country Kitchen Cookbook
Polish Cuisine, Treasury of (Bilingual)
Polish Heritage Cookery, Ill. Ed.
Polish Traditions, Old
Portuguese Encounters, Cuisines of
Pyrenees, Tastes of the
Quebec, Taste of
Rhine, All Along The
Romania, Taste of, Exp. Ed.
Russian Cooking, Best of, Exp. Ed.
Scandinavian Cooking, Best of
Scotland, Traditional Food From
Scottish-Irish Pub and Hearth Cookbook
Sephardic Israeli Cuisine
Sicilian Feasts
Smorgasbord Cooking, Best of
South American Cookery, Art of
South Indian Cooking, Healthy
Sri Lanka, Exotic Tastes of
Swedish Kitchen, A
Swiss Cookbook, The
Syria, Taste of
Taiwanese Cuisine, Best of
Thai Cuisine, Best of Regional
Turkish Cuisine, Taste of
Ukrainian Cuisine, Best of, Exp. Ed.
Uzbek Cooking, Art of
Warsaw Cookbook, Old

A Vietnamese Kitchen

Treasured Family Recipes

Ha Roda

HIPPOCRENE BOOKS
NEW YORK

Book and jacket design by Acme Klong Design, Inc.
Cover photo by Nick Wheeler.
Photography by Ha Roda.

For more information, address:
HIPPOCRENE BOOKS, INC.
171 Madison Avenue
New York, NY 10016

ISBN 0-7818-1081-7
Cataloging-in-Publication Data available from the Library of Congress.
Printed in the United States of America.

Table of Contents

Acknowledgments

I dedicate this book to my aunt, Bác Kít. These recipes are her proud creations. I am honored to have this opportunity to share them. I thank Bác Kít for being my inspiration and for helping make this cookbook possible.

My family is my pride and joy. I thank Chris, for being my number one fan, for helping me writing this book, for supporting me in all my goals, and most of all for being a wonderful husband and father. I thank my son Zephyr for being my little food tester and my daughter Thaleia for being part of my life.

I would also like to thank my sisters (Hường, Hạnh, Huệ, and Hiếu), sister-in-law (Nhi), cousins (Cô Thu, Cô Thục, Chị Sa), and friends (Jini, Antoine, Todd, Shawn, and Yuki) for testing the recipes and providing great feedback. Thank you, Mom Roda, for providing valuable suggestions and comments. Finally, I thank Bố, Mẹ, Cương, and Cường, for believing in me. I apologize if I have left anyone else out. Thank you all very much.

Introduction

Vietnamese food has been influenced by many different cuisines, including French, Chinese, and its Southeast Asian neighbors, Thailand, Cambodia, and Laos. Like the Chinese, the Vietnamese eat from a bowl with chopsticks. French sweets and pastries dominate Vietnamese desserts. *Phở*, Vietnamese Beef Noodle Soup (page 74), is unique to Vietnam. This soup is becoming well known in the United States, and is perhaps the most popular dish in Vietnamese restaurants in America.

Dishes and flavorings vary by region. The northern part of Vietnam is heavily influenced by Chinese cooking, and is known for soups and stir-fries. Vegetables are likely to be pickled in the north while they are served fresh in the south. Because of the colder climate than the south, vegetables and fruits are not as abundant in northern Vietnam as they are in the south. Northern food is mild but, as you travel further south, spiciness increases. The spiciest food is found in central Vietnam where chile peppers are common components of many dishes.

Vietnam adopted peppers and many other condiments from its Southeast Asian neighbors. Coconut milk is very popular in desserts, such as a pudding called *chè*. However, coconut milk is seldom served in main courses. Indian-style curries are occasionally prepared, including Curried Cornish Hen (page 126) or Tofu Curry (page 102).

The French had a major influence on Vietnamese food. Especially in the south, it is common to see such foods as asparagus and French bread on menus. A typical French-Vietnamese breakfast often consists of a baguette, yogurt, and orange juice. Southern Vietnamese cuisine in particular, balances many influences. One street vendor may sell noodle soup, *phở bò*, next to a vendor selling baguettes smeared with one of the many ground pork concoctions known as pâtés. Both snacks are often served with the traditional Vietnamese fish sauce, *nước chấm* or a dipping sauce made from fish sauce, sugar, lime juice, chiles, and garlic.

Vietnamese eating habits are traditionally simple and healthy. The Vietnamese eat three meals per day. Fruits are often eaten as snacks or desserts. At Vietnamese meals, all the entrées are placed on the table at the same time, served family-style. My family's motto was "You snooze, you lose." I come from a family of ten; you can imagine the feeding frenzy!

The recipes in this cookbook are basic to Vietnamese cuisine. The instructions may at times seem lengthy, but you will be rewarded with a tasty dish. The longest part of the process is usually the preparation of the ingredients; often the cooking time is quicker than for Western food. It is important to read each recipe carefully before attempting it, as some steps involve methods that are foreign to Western cooking. Handy tips and illustrations will help you throughout the book. A meal-planning guide follows the recipes, with menu suggestions for everyday and elaborate meals. Once you are comfortable preparing traditional Vietnamese food, I encourage you to modify the ingredients and menus to suit your enlightened palate.

This cookbook introduces a number of exotic ingredients. In Vietnam, pork fat, fish fat, and stomach linings are considered delicacies because fatty food displays wealth. However, as too much fat is unhealthy, this cookbook uses limited amounts of fat, and uses varieties and cuts of meat, poultry, and seafood that are familiar and readily available to Western cooks. Some recipes are vegetarian or entirely vegan.

Traditional Vietnamese food often includes monosodium glutamate (MSG). The recipes in this cookbook do not call for MSG, but be aware that commercially bottled seasonings, such as soy sauce and oyster sauce, may include MSG—read labels carefully if you want to avoid this flavoring agent.

As you will discover, Bác Kít's recipes are not only exotic but healthy, tasty, inexpensive, and easy to prepare.

About the Author

I lived in Saigon for the first ten years of my life. During this time, the Vietnam War was raging in northern Vietnam. From my point of view, life was normal until 1975 when the communist regime gained control of Vietnam, uniting the North and South. My grandparents were sponsored by St. Paul United Church of Christ and immigrated to Pekin, Illinois in search of freedom. In the summer of 1978, they sponsored my family and we joined them in Pekin. After three years, we moved to Texas for its climate and better employment opportunities.

Our happiest family times revolved around food. We created our own Vietnamese versions of American foods such as spaghetti, pizza, and hamburgers by adding fish sauce or soy sauce to the preparation. I wrote this cookbook to bridge the Vietnamese and American cultures through food. Families and friends everywhere gather around the dinner table on holidays or special occasions. Food brings everyone together. It is a language that everyone can understand.

My heritage and experiences have made me the person I am today. My Aunt Bác Kít is a retired chef and she inspired me to perfect my Vietnamese cooking. Because she has no children, Bác Kít wants to pass down her legacy of cooking to her loved ones. With the help of Bác Kít's expertise, her legacy and my goal of blending my Vietnamese heritage into a modern American lifestyle are realized in this cookbook, which documents our family's cooking. In this book, Bác Kít and I share our joy and honor of being American and our pride in being Vietnamese.

Bác Kít's Story

Kít Thị Nguyễn, known as Bác Kít or Aunt Kít to her family and friends is the chef behind this cookbook. She was born and raised in Làng Bình Cách, a small village in North Vietnam. At the age of eighteen, she moved to Saigon (now known as Hồ Chí Minh City) with her family in search of a better life. Because northerners were not always accepted in the south, the family struggled to establish themselves. They operated a convenience store for ten years, and after the fall of President Ngô Đình Diệm's regime in 1963, the family opened a wholesale rice pancake (*bánh ướt*) factory. They successfully operated the factory for more than ten years, but in 1975, my grandparents and their siblings' families, including Bác Kít emigrated to the United States.

After they arrived in Illinois, Bác Kít and her sisters were employed as cooks by the Holiday Inn in Pekin. Bác Kít quickly advanced and was ultimately promoted to head chef. Her role was to supervise the catering of all parties and special functions. She was well respected and admired by her employers. During her years at the Holiday Inn restaurant, Bác Kít experimented and created many new, enticing dishes combining American and Vietnamese flavors. Bác Kít won second place in Holiday Inn's national chef contest against thirty other contestants for her famous Chicken Burgundy (page 123).

In 1983, Bác Kít and a partner opened a French-Vietnamese restaurant called Au Bon Appétit, in Peoria, Illinois. In 1993, Bác Kít and her family moved to southern California where she became the private chef for an estate in Hollywood Hills.

Bác Kít assisted in the creation of this book for three reasons. First, to share recipes that date back as many as three generations with her many relations. Her passion and talent have always centered on cooking and she wishes to present this legacy to her loved ones. The second reason is to expose Vietnamese foods and traditions to new generations of Vietnamese Americans. As the Vietnamese express their love through food, learning more about and developing a taste for authentic Vietnamese cuisine is a valuable link to their heritage. Third, she hopes to acquaint readers with her techniques for cooking healthy and tasty Vietnamese food.

Vietnamese Culture

Vietnamese culture is so rich and vibrant that I could easily write a book about this topic alone. However, this is not my purpose here so I will discuss, only briefly, the traditions, family values, foods, economics, religions, and fashions that I grew up with. Each of these subjects varies by region, however all Vietnamese agree that food unites families and communities. Food is a source of pride and competition, and every recipe is a family secret. Love is shown through food by how much is cooked or how much is eaten.

The Vietnamese family unit is very tight. Family members support one another. Choices and decisions are determined as a unit and individualism is not highly encouraged. The firstborn child is important. A family is considered blessed if the firstborn is a boy because boys perpetuate family traditions and keep the family name alive. The oldest son and his family live with his parents until they pass away. The firstborn son inherits the role of patriarch.

The firstborn grandson of the first son is called *đích tôn. Đích* means mark or target and *tôn* means to honor. When the grandparents pass on, the son and *đích tôn* grandson accept and carry on the family's traditions. For example, they are responsible for gathering the family for such festivities as *Tết*, the Vietnamese New Year, *Giỗ*, the anniversary of the dead, and other religious ceremonies. As each family's traditions have been passed down through males from generation to generation, it is important to have a son so the traditions will live on forever.

Love is only expressed indirectly; it is understood, but kept hidden until death. Kisses and hugs between adults are considered embarrassing, but love is demonstrated via food. For example, a mother shows love through the generosity and quality of her cooking. She receives love through compliments on her food.

In courtship, the man bearing the most gifts wins the bride. Gifts come in the form of money, land, livestock, and/or gold. During earlier times, livestock and gold were common offerings to the bride's family. Today, the groom's family often gives roast pigs to the bride's family. My husband often mentions this tradition to our friends, boasting, "Yep, I bought my wife with a roasted pig." Unlike most Western weddings, at a Vietnamese wedding the groom pays for everything.

Arranged marriages used to be a common practice in Vietnam. My grandparents were married in this tradition when they were only thirteen and eleven. Sometimes marriages were arranged without the children's consent or knowledge, as the bride and groom were promised to each other before they were born, and later had to honor and obey their parents' decision. Polygamy was also accepted during my grandparents' time. My maternal grandmother found my grandfather a second wife in order to conceive a son. This action was suggested by a palm reader. My grandfather's second wife conceived a boy. Shortly after, my grandmother also gave birth to a boy, which only validated her superstition. In modern-day Vietnam, arranged marriages and polygamy are things of the past. Arranged marriages are considered old fashioned and polygamy is illegal.

Food plays an important role during holidays, including *Tết* (New Year) and *Giỗ* (the anniversary of the dead). *Bánh Chưng* and *Bánh Dày* are traditional cakes eaten during *Tết*. *Bánh Chưng* is a sticky rice cake filled with mung bean paste, ground meat, green peas, and black pepper, wrapped in green banana leaf. *Bánh Chưng* symbolizes the earth. Its ingredients are considered herbal medicines that maintain harmony between the positive and the negative helping the blood circulate and preventing diseases. *Bánh Dày* is a round sticky rice cake that symbolizes the sky. Every year during *Tết*, Vietnamese people present *Bánh Chưng* and *Bánh Dày* as special offerings to their ancestors and as special gifts to relatives and friends.

The date of *Tết* changes every year, because Vietnamese follow the Chinese lunar calendar, and the start of the lunar year is based upon the cycles of the moon. The beginning of the year can occur anywhere between late January and the middle of February. Whenever the date falls, the whole country celebrates this festival heartily for three consecutive days.

The Vietnamese observe *Giỗ* instead of birthdays. (Birthdays are celebrated during *Tết*, when everyone automatically becomes a year older.) During *Giỗ*, the head of the household offers food and paper money to the deceased. The Vietnamese believe in life after death and that the dead still enjoy food and use money. The currency is burned so the deceased will have access to it, but the living observers enjoy the food after the ceremony. *Giỗ* is a celebration for the dead, while *Tết* is a celebration of life, but both are festive occasions that unite families.

The highlight of everyday life in Vietnam is going to the open food market. Because of its wide availability, fresh produce, including exotic fruits, is served daily. Because refrigerators and microwaves are not affordable, most foods are sold and consumed within a day. Street vendors  are a dime a dozen, and sell their wares from dawn to dusk. Typically in an open market, everything can be bargained for, so individual ingredients or even an entire meal may be purchased inexpensively.

Vietnam is a poor country. America seems like heaven to many Vietnamese. The standard of living in America is definitely better than in Vietnam. However, in terms of individual wealth, some Vietnamese living in Vietnam are wealthier than Vietnamese in America. Manual labor is cheap, while merchandise manufactured in foreign countries is costly in Vietnam. Everything is paid for in cash. There is no credit in Vietnam. It is hard for an average Vietnamese to buy a new house if he or she does not have the cash for it. Almost everyone owns a small business. For some Vietnamese, the back of the building is their living quarters while the front is used for business. Businesses are typically passed down through generations. Life is not kind to the poor in Vietnam. If an individual starts out with nothing, his or her chance to own a business is very slim.

The most popular organized religions in Vietnam are Buddhism and Catholicism. Some households, such as my godparents', respected both religions. They had statues of both Buddha and Mary in their living room in order to be on the good side of both religions. Regardless of

faith, most Vietnamese follow the philosophies of Confucianism and Taoism as a way of life. They believe what goes around comes around, and so they lend a helping hand. Someday, when they need help, someone will lend them a helping hand.

Superstition is almost a religion of its own. Most Vietnamese believe in ghosts, the afterlife, that black cats bring bad luck, and things that go bump in the night. My godmother believed I was her reincarnated daughter, who died at the age of ten. She had a dream, in which she was told that her daughter had been reincarnated. The following day, my paternal grandmother brought me to my godmother's home. My grandmother complained that I was a difficult baby to care for. My parents were working. No one else would baby-sit me. I cried constantly, but I stopped as soon as my godmother picked me up. We became inseparable. When my parents moved away taking me with them, I pined for my godmother. It broke my mother's heart to see me so sad, so I lived with my godparents during the week and visited my parents on the weekend for the next ten years. Whether I am really my godmother's reincarnated daughter, I will never know. Somehow, deep down, I believe her.

The traditional Vietnamese dress is called *áo dài*. It elegantly emphasizes the gentle and curvaceous shape of Vietnamese women. Teenage schoolgirls wear white *áo dài* uniforms. Women wear *áo dài* for special events such as weddings, parties, and *Tết*. This style of dress is also worn as a uniform by government employees. The *áo dài* contributes a unique look to Vietnamese fashion, and will probably continue to be worn in that country for many years to come.

My aunt taught me an interesting phrase, *"Cái răng cái tóc là góc con người."* Roughly translated it means, "Teeth and hair make a person." It is an insightful statement. A great smile with nice teeth goes a long way. But the phrase carries an additional meaning for Vietnamese: Before 1930, black teeth were considered fashionable in North Vietnam. Men and women dyed their teeth black. The women's ebony black teeth, rosy cheeks, and ruby lips attracted many men. This tradition faded away after the French influence, but my grandmother died with a perfect set of black teeth.

A Vietnamese Kitchen

Vietnamese is harsh on women, despite the fact that they are generally the breadwinners of the family. Some physical attributes, such as fairness or slight chubbiness are status symbols. If a woman has a pale complexion, she is considered beautiful; this coloring is associated with the upper class. Dark skin, on the other hand, symbolizes the poor working class, many of whom get tan working in the rice fields all day. Even if her complexion is merely the result of genetics, a dark-skinned woman will be looked down upon. Chubbiness symbolizes wealth: If a family is slightly overweight, they have  money to eat well. Ironically, in America, many poor people have weight problems, due to a diet high in fats and sweets, while slimness is considered fashionable. In this last regard, Bác Kít's recipes bridge both cultures, producing elegant, yet inexpensive meals that don't add pounds.

Vietnam's Culinary Culture

Although in many ways Vietnam is similar to China, it maintains its own identity through its food. Many Westerners, however, confuse Vietnamese cuisine with that of Thailand. In general, Vietnamese food is less spicy, but in both cultures meals are very simple, usually consisting of a soup, a stir-fry, and plain rice. This chapter will discuss primary ingredients, dining etiquette, foods special to each region, and the adaptability of Vietnamese food to its environment.

Rice and fish sauce are the primary elements of Vietnamese cuisine. Rice is the easiest grain to grow in Vietnam. It is cheap and used in many dishes. It is processed into rice flour to make many items such as *bánh đa* (rice paper), *bún* (rice noodles), and rice flour-based desserts. There are many kinds of rice in Vietnam, including regular white rice, jasmine rice, sweet (or sticky) rice called *gạo nếp*, and broken rice. Each has its own characteristics. Regular white rice is eaten in most Vietnamese homes at every meal. Jasmine rice is moister and has a wonderfully sweet fragrance. It is eaten by the upper class at every meal. The shorter-grained *gạo nếp* is steamed into *xôi* (sweet rice) with various other ingredients, such as mung beans, coconuts, and sugar, and is eaten at breakfast or as dessert. Broken rice is steamed into *cơm tấm* (page 62), and served in restaurants for breakfast.

Vietnam is bound by the South China Sea and thus enjoys a plethora of seafood, and fish sauce is the most popular Vietnamese flavoring. It is made from different kinds of fish, but anchovy-based sauce is the tastiest.

Making fish sauce is a lengthy process. As a little girl, Bác Kít's mother taught her how to make at home. Fish was layered with cooked rice, sweet rice wine, and salt. This was left to ferment for at least thirty days. A batch of fermented fish creates three grades of fish sauce. The first extraction is called *nước mắm nhỉ*. After the liquid is extracted, water and salt are added to what remains, and cooked for at least one hour. The liquid extracted from this batch is called *nước mắm nhất*. After the liquid has been extracted from the second batch, more water and salt are added. The third batch is cooked for at least one more hour, to produce *nước mắm*. Each type is cooked with additional ingredients, such as sugar and salt. Homemade or bottled commercially, *nước mắm nhỉ* is the best tasting of the three. *Nước mắm nhất* is less pungent and thinner than *nước mắm nhỉ*, which is also very good. Upper-class Vietnamese people use *nước mắm nhỉ* as a dipping sauce, although some prefer *nước mắm nhất*, which is widely used by middle-class Vietnamese. *nước mắm* is the cheapest and is used primarily for cooking.

Growing up, we had to follow a certain dining etiquette, which was more complex than the contents of the meal itself. The father is the head of the household. He consumes an appetizer, such as a boiled chicken leg or chicken gizzards, with a glass of fine rice wine while the rest of the family waits patiently. Starting with the youngest, children invite their older siblings and parents to start the meal. This custom of invitation is called *mời*. The father is always the first person to taste a dish. When the meal is done, the children politely excuse themselves. The oldest girl clears the dishes.

Bác Kít discovered the culinary specialties of Vietnam's regions when her family migrated to southern Vietnam. The northern Vietnamese specialties include Northern Beef Noodle Soup, *Phở Bắc* (page 74); Shrimp Noodle Soup, *Bún Riêu* (page 84); Fish or Shrimp Stew, *Kho cá* or *Tôm* (page 116 or 118); and boiled spinach, *luộc rau muống*. The central Vietnamese claim to fame is Huế-style Beef Noodle Soup, *Bún Bò Huế* (page 76). Huế, known for its spicy food, is the major city of central Vietnam, and Huế-style Beef Noodle Soup is a very spicy soup. It differs from the northern variation because the noodles are thinner and the broth is spicier. Beef vinegar hot pot, *Thịt Bò Nhúng Dấm* (page 130), wrapped in fresh vegetables and herbs is a southern region specialty.

Most northern and central Vietnamese are farmers. Annual storms and floods cause Vietnamese farmers to be frugal. They adapt to their environment and ration their food for rainy days, literally. Similarly, Bác Kít had to adapt to a new culture when she came to America. American supermarkets did not stock Vietnamese ingredients, although most items may be found at Asian groceries. She adapted her recipes to what was available, replicating flavors and textures as best she could.

Sauces and Condiments

Sauces and condiments play an important role in Vietnamese cooking because most dishes rely primarily on them, rather than the components of a dish for flavor. Fish sauce is a very important condiment used by most Vietnamese, available at every meal as a condiment or as a dipping sauce.

I introduced my husband, Chris, to fish sauce when we first met. He enjoyed the taste so much that he added it to every Vietnamese dish he came across. One day, he stumbled upon Crumpled Sweet Rice, *Xôi Vò* (page 150). Of course, Chris was adamant on adding fish sauce to this dessert. After tasting the fish sauce with crumpled sweet rice, he turned to me with the cutest frown on his face. Learning it the hard way, Chris realized that fish sauce does not taste good with everything, especially not desserts.

The central and southern parts of Vietnam serve very spicy food whereas the North serves mild food. Someone once told me, "The hotter the climate, the spicier the food." This may be because spices generate sweat to cool body temperatures. I am personally not a flame-eater and this cookbook contains very few spicy dishes. If you prefer your dishes to be hotter, add your favorite chiles to the sauces and condiments to give your taste buds a pleasurable zing.

Fifteen to twenty years ago, certain condiments were not available in the United States, but most are now available in many supermarkets and Asian groceries. The following recipes are the fundamental building blocks for great Vietnamese sauces. Feel free to modify the ingredients according to your taste. Have fun and experiment.

Anchovy Sauce

Mắm Nêm

Makes 1½ cups

This recipe is a doctored version of a bottled mắm nêm, *a popular dipping sauce in southern Vietnam. It is a pungent condiment that needs to be diluted before serving . The combination of anchovy sauce, garlic, lemongrass, and pineapple yields a distinctive flavor and scent.* Mắm nêm *is served with such dishes as Spring Rolls (page 31), Beef Vinegar Hot Pot (page 130), and Sautéed Shrimp (page 141). Anchovy lovers will flip head over heels for this sauce.*

2 teaspoons finely chopped lemongrass

1 teaspoon minced garlic

¼ cup canned crushed pineapple, drained

½ cup bottled anchovy sauce (mắm nêm)

3 tablespoons granulated sugar

⅓ cup rice vinegar

In a small bowl, combine the lemongrass, garlic, and pineapple. Mix well.

In a saucepan, combine the anchovy sauce, sugar, vinegar, ⅓ cup of water, and half of the lemongrass mixture. Cook over low heat for 5 minutes. Remove the saucepan from the heat and allow the mixture to cool completely, about 30 to 60 minutes. Stir in the remaining lemongrass mixture.

Spicy Lemon Fish Sauce

Nước Mắm Chanh ớt

Makes ½ cup

Nước mắm chanh ớt *is used as dipping sauce for many Vietnamese foods, such as boiled vegetables, meats, and omelets. The spicy flavors give your food an extra zing. This recipe maybe be easily halved or doubled.*

¼ cup fish sauce

1 teaspoon finely chopped fresh ginger

1 teaspoon minced garlic

½ teaspoon finely chopped Thai pepper

2 tablespoons lemon juice

4 teaspoons sugar

In a small bowl, combine the fish sauce, ginger, garlic, chili pepper, lemon juice, and sugar. Mix well. Cover and refrigerate until needed.

Sweet-and-Sour Fish Sauce

Nước Mắm Ngọt

Nước mắm ngọt is used as a condiment for such dishes as Egg Rolls (page 32), Spring Rolls (page 31), Rice or Noodle Grilled Pork (pages 78 and 80), and Beef Vinegar Hot Pot (page 130). The sweet-and-sour taste compliments many meat dishes.

1 cup fish sauce

1 cup sugar

⅓ cup rice vinegar

1 teaspoon finely chopped garlic

1 teaspoon crushed Thai pepper (optional)

In a medium-size saucepan, combine the fish sauce, sugar, vinegar, and 4 cups of water over high heat. Bring to a boil, then remove from the heat and stir in the garlic and pepper.

Allow the mixture to cool completely, at least 30 to 60 minutes. Cover and refrigerate until ready to serve.

Tip: This sauce may be stored in the refrigerator for several months.

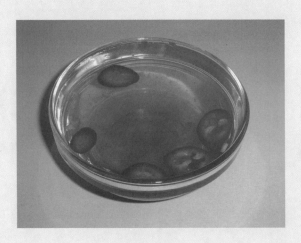

Browning Sauce

Kẹo Ðắng

Kẹo đắng *is sugar melted into a dark and bittersweet sauce. It is used primarily for coloring* kho *dishes, to which it adds a subtle sweetness and bitterness. This is a very simple recipe. Anyone can whip it up in just a few minutes.*

Warning: Turn on all your vents and open all your windows. Smoke from the sugar might otherwise set off your smoke alarms. Please read the entire recipe through before starting.

1 cup sugar

Cook the sugar in a small saucepan for 1 to 2 minutes over high heat, or until it melts, bubbles and turns dark brown like molasses. It is normal for the sugar to smoke.

Reduce the heat to medium-low. Slowly add ¾ cup of water. Be careful—the water will splatter because of the heat. Cook, stirring for 30 seconds, or until the sugar dissolves. Remove the saucepan from the heat.

This sauce can be used to enhance the color and the texture of most Vietnamese *kho* dishes, such as Catfish Pepper Stew (page 116), Pork Stew (page 114), and Egg and Pork Stew (page 115).

Sweet-and-Sour Hoisin Sauce

Tương Ngọt

Makes 1½ cups

Tương ngọt *is a sweet-and-sour dipping sauce. It is used as a condiment for such foods as Egg Rolls (page 32), Spring Rolls (page 31), Beef Vinegar Hot Pot (page 130), and Vietnamese Meatballs (page 133). This dipping sauce is frequently used as a mild substitute for Anchovy Sauce (page 21).*

1 cup hoisin sauce

¼ cup rice vinegar

1 teaspoon peanut butter

½ cup pineapple or fresh orange juice

1 teaspoon crushed Thai pepper (optional)

In a small saucepan, combine the hoisin sauce, vinegar, peanut butter, and pineapple. Bring to a boil over medium-high heat. Remove the saucepan from the heat and stir in the Thai pepper. Allow the mixture to cool for 30 to 60 minutes, then refrigerate until ready to serve.

Pickled Mustard Greens

Dưa Chua

Dưa chua is comparable to American pickles. It is commonly served with stewed dishes, rice, and fish sauce-based condiments, such as Spicy Lemon Fish Sauce (page 22). Dưa chua tastes great in soups or stir-fries. Refrigerated, the pickled greens keep for one month.

---

3 pounds Chinese mustard greens (dưa cải)

3 tablespoons salt

2 tablespoons sugar

½ cup rice vinegar

1 medium-size onion, thinly sliced

1 gallon-size container with lid

Spread the mustard greens on a baking sheet and leave them in the sun to dry for 2 hours, or until the leaves wilt. Chop the wilted leaves into ½- to 1-inch lengths.

In a large saucepan, combine the salt, sugar, vinegar, and 10 cups of water. Bring to a boil and then remove the saucepan from the heat. Allow the mixture to cool completely, then pour it into the 1-gallon container.

Add the mustard greens and onion to the pickling liquid. Close the container tightly with its lid. Allow the mixture to pickle at room temperature. If the room is warm, allow the mixture to pickle for at least 2 days. If cold, allow the mixture to pickle for at least 3 to 4 days. The longer they pickle, the sourer the mustard greens become. Once the desired sourness is reached, place the pickled mustard greens in the refrigerator.

Before serving, drain the desired amount of greens. (You may wish to reserve the juice to use in soups.) If the pickled greens are too sour, rinse them in cold water.

Pickled Eggs

Trứng Muối

Pickled eggs look like raw eggs, however, the taste is different. The yolk yields a rich and buttery flavor. The egg white may be salty but it is still edible.

They are great in Egg and Pork Stew (page 115) and the yolks are used in moon cakes (bánh trung thu), which are eaten during the Mid-Autumn Moon Festival known as Tết Trung Thu. The cake is filled with lotus seeds, mung beans, and orange peel. The yolk is placed in the center of the cake to represent the moon. It is my favorite part of the whole cake.

1 cup salt

1 dozen eggs

1 gallon container with lid

Bring 6 cups of water to a boil over high heat. Add the salt and stir until completely dissolved. Remove from the heat. Allow the salt water to cool to room temperature.

When cool, pour the salt water into the container. Label the container with the date. Place the eggs in the salt water and soak at room temperature for at least 1 month. Keep the container tightly closed with a lid. The longer they soak, the saltier the eggs become.

When the eggs are ready, they must be boiled. Serve with Steamed Rice (page 61).

Appetizers

Appetizers were not popular in Vietnam until the French introduced the concept of separate courses. Even today, appetizers are mainly served in restaurants, not in homes where many dishes are served at
the same time and shared at the table. In fact, I did not know about
appetizers until I moved to America.

Occasionally during festive occasions, chicken gizzards and hearts or
cow tongues are served as appetizers. These delicacies are usually
served with beer or wine for the adults. Finger foods such as Egg Rolls
(page 32), Spring Rolls (page 31), and Vietnamese Meatballs (page 133)
are served for the children. Gizzards and hearts were not my favorites
when I was younger, however, as I grew older I developed a nostalgic
taste for these delicacies.

During *Tết*, different appetizers are served all day long. Soups, stir-fries,
meat and *kho* dishes, and steamed rice are also served. The room is
filled with laughter and loud voices yelling across the table. The feast
goes on for hours, sometimes all day. By the end of the meal, everyone
is too full for dessert. However, fresh fruits such as oranges, watermel-
on, and seasoned fruits are always available for those who still have a
little room left. In my opinion, it is an experience that everyone should
enjoy at least once. It is a blast! I am digressing. Writing about my experience is getting me excited and hungry.

While Vietnamese cuisine does not include a category for appetizers,
Vietnamese feasts are filled with lots of finger foods. In a strange way,
these are actually appetizers but we never classify them as such. Feasts
seldom occur so the concept of appetizers is rarely considered. This
chapter contains recipes for typical Vietnamese snacks and finger foods
which may be served as appetizers.

Spring Rolls

Gỏi Cuốn

Makes 16 spring rolls

Gỏi cuốn are great appetizers because they are light and simple. Since the ingredients are mostly vegetables, the food does not feel heavy in your stomach and leaves room for the main dish—provided you do not eat too many spring rolls. The ingredients are wrapped in rice paper, then dipped into Sweet-and-Sour Hoisin Sauce (page 25) or Anchovy Sauce (page 21). There are many ways to prepare spring rolls. This recipe uses shrimp and pork, but you may substitute chicken and crabmeat, for example. Have fun and be creative!

---

1 pound shrimp

½ cup lemon juice

½ pound boneless pork

½ (16-ounce) package rice stick noodles (bún), cooked (page 64)

½ head lettuce, torn into bite-size pieces

½ pound bean sprouts

½ bunch mint

½ bunch cilantro, stemmed

1 (12-ounce) package rice paper (bánh tráng)

Boil the shrimp in 1 cup of water and the lemon juice until the shrimp turns pink. Remove the saucepan from the heat. Shell and devein the shrimp (page 120).

In a saucepan, boil the pork with 6 cups of water over medium-high heat for 15 minutes, or until no longer pink. Remove the saucepan from the heat. Transfer the pork to a bowl and allow it to cool. Cut the pork into thin slices.

Separate the rice papers from each other. Fill a large bowl with hot water. Briefly dip each rice paper into the bowl until it is just slightly wet. Oversoaking the rice paper will make wrapping difficult.

Place the rice paper flat on a plate. Layer the ingredients in the center of the rice paper in the following order: a small piece of lettuce, 10 to 20 rice noodles, 5 or 6 bean sprouts, a sprig of mint, and a few cilantro leaves. Place three pieces of shrimp side by side on top. Place three pork slivers in between the shrimp.

Wrap all the ingredients spring roll-style (appendix, page 163).

Egg Rolls
Chả Giò

Makes 40 to 50 egg rolls

Everyone has a different way of preparing egg rolls or, chả giò. *Bác Kít's are crunchy outside, yet soft with a balanced amount of meat and vegetables inside.*

There are three ways to eat egg rolls. The first is simply to eat them as a finger food. The second is to prepare them in a vegetable wrap: the egg rolls are cut into bite-size pieces, which are each wrapped in lettuce with several strands of rice noodles and a few cilantro leaves, and then dipped in Sweet-and-Sour Fish Sauce (page 23). Finally, the egg rolls can be cut into bite-size pieces, and served over rice noodles with lettuce, cilantro, bean sprouts, and Sweet-and-Sour Fish Sauce.

60 frozen square egg roll wrappers (such as TYJ Spring Roll Pastry), thawed

1 (1.8-ounce) package bean thread noodles (miến)

½ cup chopped dried black mushrooms

3 carrots, peeled and roughly chopped

1 head cabbage, roughly chopped

½ medium-size onion, roughly chopped

1 pound ground pork

1 pound ground chicken

1 tablespoon salt

¼ teaspoon black pepper

2 eggs

1 teaspoon all purpose flour

3 cups vegetable oil

Soak the dried noodles and mushrooms in separate bowls of hot water for approximately 10 minutes.

Finely chop the carrots, cabbage, and onion in a food processor, pulsing several times until the vegetables are minced. With a clean kitchen towel, squeeze out all the liquid. (This prevents the egg rolls from being soggy.) Place the vegetable mixture in a large bowl.

Drain the noodles and cut them into 1- to 2-inch lengths. Drain the mushrooms. In a bowl, combine the noodles, mushrooms, pork, chicken, salt, pepper, and eggs with the ground vegetables.

In a small bowl, mix the flour and 2 teaspoons of water into a paste, which will be used to seal the egg rolls. Peel the egg roll wrappers apart. You can peel the skins as you go, but I find it much faster to separate them all before wrapping. Set 1 wrapper on a large plate, with 1 corner facing you. Place 1 heaping tablespoon of the filling in

A Vietnamese Kitchen

the center of the wrapper, then spread the mixture 2 1/2 to 3 inches from the center toward the far corner of the wrapper. Flip the corner nearest you over the mixture, to form a triangle. Fold the left and right corners evenly over the first fold, to form a tight cylindrical package.

Roll the folded egg roll away from you, ensuring that any loose ends are neatly tucked inside. The roll should be firm, to prevent the mixture from escaping during frying. Thinly spread the flour paste on the underside of the last corner of the wrapper to secure it (appendix, page 164).

Heat the oil in a deep fryer or a deep nonstick frying pan for 1 to 2 minutes over medium heat. Do not allow the oil to become too hot or the outside of the egg rolls will burn before the inside cooks. A deep fryer will maintain a constant temperature, and thus is preferable to a frying pan. Dip the corner of an egg roll into the oil to test the temperature. When the oil sizzles, fry the egg rolls in batches of no more than 10 (do not overfill the fryer). Fry each batch for 15 to 20 minutes, or until golden brown. Transfer the cooked egg rolls to a plate lined with paper towels to absorb excess oil.

Tips: Wrapped egg rolls can be frozen until ready to be fried. Place the uncooked egg rolls side by side in large freezer bags immediately after they have been wrapped. When ready to fry, do not thaw the egg rolls. Place the frozen egg rolls directly into the hot oil. (This prevents the egg rolls from becoming soggy.)

After frying a large quantity of egg rolls for 15 to 20 minutes, many burnt flakes and crumbs blacken the oil in the frying pan. If you do not own a deep fryer, one way to avoid blackened egg rolls is to strain the oil when the oil darkens or contains many burnt crumbs.

Sautéed Meat Patties

Chả Chiên   *4 servings*

Chả *refers to a meat patty that makes a great finger food. The next three recipes are all for* chả, *cooked in three different ways.* Chả chiên *is fried,* chả lụa *(opposite page) is boiled, and* chả quế *(page 36) is roasted. The meat in* chả *(usually pork) is marinated with spices.* Chả chiên *is crispy on the outside and moist on the inside. This patty can be served plain, with rice, or bread.*

---

1 pound boneless pork or 1 pound ground pork, beef, chicken, or turkey

1 teaspoon baking powder

5 teaspoons fish sauce

1 teaspoon sugar

1 tablespoon potato flakes

2 cups plus 2 tablespoons vegetable oil

⅛ teaspoon black pepper

If the meat has not been ground, trim the fat and chop it into small chunks. In a bowl, combine the meat, baking powder, fish sauce, sugar, potato flakes, vegetable oil, black pepper, and 1 tablespoon of water. Cover and refrigerate for at least 6 hours.

In a food processor, finely grind the meat for 1 minute. Work the meat from the bottom of the processor to the top with a spatula or a spoon. Grind for 1 minute longer. Transfer to a bowl. Cover and refrigerate until ready to cook.

Place the meat in a plastic bag. With clean hands, knead it in the plastic for 1 minute and then shape it into a ball. Remove it from the plastic bag. Form the meat into 4 balls. Flatten each ball into a patty.

Heat the remaining 2 cups of oil in a nonstick frying pan for 2 minutes over medium-high heat. Place the patties into the frying pan. Flip the patties frequently to cook evenly, until the meat is no longer pink. Transfer the patties to a dish lined with paper towels and blot the excess oil with the paper towels. Allow the patties to cool. Serve with steamed rice (page 61), on bread as a sandwich, or as an appetizer.

Tip: You may freeze unground marinated meat for several weeks in the freezer. Thaw the meat before continuing with the recipe.

Banana Leaf Meat Patties

Chả Lụa

4 to 6 servings

Chả lụa is a boiled meatloaf. Any type of meat will do, however, pork is most common. Traditionally, chả lụa is wrapped tightly in banana leaves, which yield a faint green color and a subtle banana flavor to the meat. Unfortunately, banana leaves are not available everywhere, so this recipe may be prepared without them. Chả lụa's texture is similar to bologna and it is flavorful in every bite.

---

1 recipe Sautéed Meat Patties (page 34), prepared through kneading

Kitchen twine

3 (28 x 9-inch) pieces of aluminum foil

1 medium-size banana leaf, big enough to cover the meat (optional)

Shape the meat into a 6-inch-long loaf and wrap tightly in a plastic bag.

Stack the pieces of foil on top of each other and place the banana leaf on top. Remove the meat from the bag. Place the meat at 1 short end of the foil, and roll up tightly. Fold both ends of the foil tightly and neatly against the meat. Press each end against a flat surface 2 or 3 times to compress and flatten it.

Wrap the twine tightly around the loaf twice lengthwise and widthwise. Tie the ends and trim the excess.

Bring 10 to 12 cups of water to a boil in a large saucepan over medium-high heat. Use enough water to keep the loaf afloat. Add the loaf, then cover and cook for 45 minutes.

Remove the saucepan from the heat. Transfer the meatloaf to a dish. Allow it to cool for 30 minutes. Remove the foil and banana leaf before serving. Serve slices of *chả lụa* with steamed rice, on bread as a sandwich, or as an appetizer.

Tip: You may freeze the unprocessed marinated meat for several weeks. When ready to cook, transfer the frozen meat to the refrigerator to thaw.

Roasted Cinnamon Meat Patty

Chả Quế

4 to 6 servings

Chả quế *is definitely the easiest to make of the three* chả *dishes. This dish consists of meat flavored with cinnamon and other seasonings. Cinnamon is a common ingredient in Vietnamese meat dishes. As with the other* chả *recipes, pork is traditionally used, but any kind of meat will work. In the old days,* chả quế *was prepared rotisserie-style over an open fire. Today, ovens are more practical.*

1 recipe Sautéed Meat Patties (page 34), prepared through kneading with ½ teaspoon ground cinnamon

Preheat the oven to 350°F. Wrap the meat in plastic wrap. Knead it in the plastic for 1 minute and gently shape it into a large ball. Flatten the ball into a 1-inch-thick patty. Wet your hands slightly with water before handling the meat, to prevent the mixture from sticking to your hands.

Remove the plastic wrap and place the patty in an ungreased 9 x 13-inch pan. Bake for 20 minutes. Turn the oven to broil on HIGH. With the oven door open, rotate the pan once a minute to cook evenly. Broil for 5 minutes, or until the meat is golden brown. Do not overcook, or the patty will be tough. Slice into 2- to 3-inch squares. Serve with Steamed Rice (page 61), on bread as a sandwich, or alone as an appetizer.

Tip: You may use aluminum foil in place of a baking pan for less cleaning. Be sure to shape the foil to mimic a deep baking pan. This will catch any overflowed meat juice.

Meat Omelets

Chả Trứng   *Makes 6 to 8 small pancakes*

This simple recipe is a good way to use up leftover meat and vegetables. It was passed on from my grandmother to my mom and aunts, and then to me. My grandmother always complained about how much food we wasted. Now, when my mom or aunts visit, they take over the kitchen: nothing in the refrigerator is left untouched. Chả trứng brings leftovers back to life with new, interesting flavors.

½ ounce bean thread noodles (miến)

¼ cup chopped dried black mushrooms

3 ounces ground pork, beef, chicken, or turkey

3 eggs

½ cup finely chopped onion

¼ cup finely chopped green onion

1 cup finely shredded cabbage or bean sprouts

1 tablespoon fish sauce

¼ teaspoon salt

⅛ teaspoon black pepper

½ cup vegetable oil

Soak the noodles and dried mushrooms in separate bowls of hot water for 10 minutes. Drain and chop the noodles into small pieces. Drain the mushrooms. In a large bowl, combine the noodles and mushrooms with the pork, eggs, onion, green onion, cabbage, fish sauce, salt, and pepper. Mix well.

Heat the oil in a large frying pan over medium-high heat for 2 to 3 minutes. Spoon 1 heaping tablespoon of the batter into the pan. Flatten the batter with a spatula.
Cook each omelet for 2 minutes, or until the batter sets. Flip the omelets and cook for 2 minutes. Flip once more, reduce the heat to medium-low, and cook for 2 more minutes or until browned.

Transfer the omelets to a dish lined with paper towels to blot excess grease from the pancakes. Continue cooking the batter until all the pancakes have been fried.

Spicy Lemon Fish Sauce (page 22) or plain fish sauce is an ideal condiment for these pancakes. Serve with Steamed Rice (page 61) or as an appetizer.

Beer-Battered Veggies

Nấm Hành Tẩm Bột Chiên   *2 to 4 servings*

This recipe is a good vegetarian alternative to beer battered shrimp (page 39). For a crunchier crust, make sure the vegetables are completely covered with bread crumbs and fry them until golden.

1 (12-ounce) can beer

2 eggs, lightly beaten

½ teaspoon salt

⅛ teaspoon black pepper

1¾ cups all-purpose flour

3 cups dry bread crumbs

8 ounces mushrooms, quartered

1 onion, thinly sliced

1 bell pepper, seeded and cut into 16 wedges

1 zucchini, thinly sliced

4 cups vegetable oil

Combine the beer, eggs, salt, and pepper in a bowl. Slowly mix in the flour, stirring to break up any lumps. The batter should not be too runny or too thick.

Pour the bread crumbs into a flat tray. Dip the vegetables into the batter and then in the crumbs. Lay the vegetables in a single layer on a baking sheet. Repeat the process until all the vegetables are coated.

Heat the oil in a deep frying pan or deep fryer. Fry the vegetables for 2 to 4 minutes or until golden.

Beer-Battered Shrimp

Tôm Tẩm Bột Chiên

2 to 4 servings

Beer-battered shrimp is a fun and crunchy finger food. It is a great dish for kids, my children love them. Before my grandmother passed away, her house had always been one of my favorite places to visit because of the plethora of beer-battered shrimp.

2 pounds shrimp
1 (12-ounce) can beer
2 eggs, lightly beaten
½ teaspoon salt
⅛ teaspoon black pepper
1¾ cups all-purpose flour
2 cups dry bread crumbs
4 cups vegetable oil

Peel and clean the shrimp, leaving the tail intact. The tail is used as a handle to dip the shrimp into the batter.

Combine the beer, eggs, salt, and pepper in a bowl. Slowly mix in the flour, stirring to break up any lumps. The batter should not be too runny or too thick.

Pour the bread crumbs onto a flat tray. Dip the shrimp into the batter then in the crumbs. Place the shrimp on a baking sheet in a single layer. Repeat the process until all the shrimp are coated.

Heat the oil in a deep frying pan or a deep fryer. Fry the shrimp for 3 to 5 minutes or until lightly golden.

Soup and Salad

Rice and noodles are staples of every Vietnamese meal. To many Americans, soup and salad makes a light meal, but to a Vietnamese, a meal without rice or noodles is not a complete meal. One can be full right after eating them, but will be hungry again in an hour. The starchiness in rice or noodles keeps you full longer and lasts you until the next meal. The Vietnamese usually fill a bowl with rice first and add soup or salad on top.

Traditionally, lettuce and other vegetables are used in wraps such as Spring Rolls (page 31). Other than Vietnamese Coleslaw (page 55), very few salads are common. In southern Vietnam, however, the French expanded the salad repertoire in many restaurants. Some salads are great as appetizers while others are good entrées, such as Saigon Beef Salad (page 56).

Most Vietnamese meals includes soup. Believe it or not, in Vietnam no one drinks beverages during a meal except on special occasions. They drink before or after a meal but not during. In my opinion, soup is the substitute for a beverage.

Most of the recipes in this chapter are everyday dishes that are dependent on other entrées to make a full Vietnamese meal. Elaborate soups and salads, such as Sweet-and-Sour Catfish Soup (page 50) and Saigon Beef (page 56), are reserved for special festivities such as family gatherings or the anniversary of the dead.

Bok Choy Soup

Canh Cải Ngọt

4 servings

Canh cải ngọt *is very simple to make. This soup contains ground meat (pork, beef, chicken, or turkey), bok choy, cilantro, and an accent of ginger. You may replace bok choy with other leafy green vegetables, such as mustard greens.*

1 tablespoon vegetable oil

6 ounces meat (any kind), thinly sliced

2 tablespoons finely chopped onion

1 pound bok choy or baby bok choy, chopped into 1-inch pieces

1 tablespoon fish sauce

1 teaspoon salt

1 teaspoon mushroom seasoning (optional)

1 teaspoon finely chopped fresh ginger

1 tablespoon finely chopped fresh cilantro

Heat the oil in a saucepan and stir-fry the meat and onion for 3 to 5 minutes over high heat. Stir in 4 cups of water, the fish sauce, salt, and mushroom seasoning. Bring to a boil, then reduce the heat to medium-low and cook for 10 minutes. Add the bok choy and increase the heat to medium-high. Cook for 5 minutes.

Remove the saucepan from the heat. Add the ginger and cilantro to the soup. Serve with Steamed Rice (page 61).

Eggplant Chowder
Canh Cà

Roasting is a common Vietnamese way of cooking eggplant; however, it can get boring. Canh cà *offers a refreshing new way to prepare eggplant. It is served as an appetizer or an entrée with rice. This soup is light and delicious.*

¼ (4-ounce)package tofu

½ cup vegetable oil

2 teaspoons finely minced garlic

¼ cup finely chopped green onion

¼ cup finely chopped fresh cilantro

½ cup mung beans

6 ounces ground meat, marinated (page 132)

¼ cup finely chopped onion

1 teaspoon salt

1 tablespoon fish sauce

2 to 3 long purple eggplants (1 pound), cut diagonally into 1-inch slices

1 medium-size tomato, cut into wedges

⅛ teaspoon black pepper

¼ cup chopped tía tô mint (optional)

Soak the tofu in a bowl of hot water for 15 to 20 minutes. This will help make it firm. Slice the tofu into 1 x 2-inch rectangles. Drain on paper towels for at least 5 minutes. Heat the oil in a large frying pan over medium-high heat. Fry the tofu until lightly golden. Transfer to a plate and use paper towels to absorb the excess oil. Slice the tofu into ⅛- to ¼-inch strips and set aside.

In a bowl, combine the garlic, green onion, cilantro, and mint. Set aside. Rinse the mung beans in a strainer. In a saucepan, bring 2 cups of water to a boil over medium-high heat. Add the mung beans. Cook for 5 minutes. Remove the saucepan from the heat. Drain, rinse, and redrain the mung beans and set aside.

Using the same saucepan, cook the meat over medium-high heat for 4 to 5 minutes, or until no longer pink. Add 5 cups of water and mix well. Add the mung beans, onion, salt, and fish sauce, and cook for 5 minutes. Skim off any foam. Reduce the heat to medium and cook for 5 minutes. Add the eggplant, tomato, and tofu. Partly cover the saucepan with a lid and cook for 15 more minutes.

Remove the saucepan from the heat. Add the cilantro, green onion, and the garlic mixture. Sprinkle black pepper over the chowder. Taste the broth and adjust with additional salt or water if necessary. Serve as an appetizer or with Steamed Rice (page 61).

Tip: The tofu is sliced both before and after frying because is much easier to fry a large piece of tofu then small pieces, which often crumble when fried.

Potato Soup

Canh Khoai Tây

Because of its starchy content, potato soup is not as light as tofu soup (page 49). I was not a fan of leafy green vegetables when I was little, so I have fond childhood memories of this soup.

1 tablespoon vegetable oil

1 teaspoon minced garlic

½ onion, cut into 6 wedges

6 ounces ground or thinly sliced beef, chicken, or pork, marinated (page 132)

3 red potatoes, peeled and cut into bite-size pieces

½ teaspoon salt

1 tablespoon fish sauce

¼ cup finely chopped fresh cilantro

1 tablespoon finely chopped green onion

⅛ teaspoon black pepper

Heat the oil in a saucepan over medium-high heat. Add the garlic and onion and sauté, stirring, until lightly golden. Add the meat and sauté for 1 minute or until no longer pink.

Pour 5 cups of water into the saucepan and bring to a boil. Add the potatoes and return to a boil. Mix in the salt and fish sauce. Reduce the heat to medium and cook for 10 minutes or until the potato is tender. Adjust with additional salt if necessary.

Remove from the heat. Sprinkle the cilantro, green onion, and black pepper over the soup. Serve with Steamed Rice (page 61).

Stuffed Squash Soup

Canh Bí Nhồi

4 servings

Canh bí nhồi contains zucchini in chicken broth. The squash is stuffed with ground pork, glass noodles, mushrooms, and seasonings. It is a warm and refreshing soup for a cold winter day.

¼ cup chopped dried black mushrooms

½ cup bean thread noodles (miến)

4 ounces ground pork, marinated (page 132)

1 egg

2 tablespoons finely chopped onion

⅛ teaspoon black pepper

2 medium zucchini

½ teaspoon salt

1 cube chicken-flavored bouillon or 1 cup chicken broth

¼ cup finely chopped green onion

¼ cup finely chopped fresh cilantro

Soak the mushrooms and noodles in separate bowls of hot water for 10 minutes. Drain. Cut the noodles into 1-inch lengths.

In a bowl, combine the meat with the mushrooms, noodles, egg, onion, and black pepper. Peel the zucchini and slice it into 2-inch rounds. Use a spoon to scrape out the seeds from the center of the zucchini. Stuff the meat mixture into the centers.

Bring 6 cups of water and the chicken broth to a boil over high heat (If using chicken broth, use only 5 cups of water). Add the salt and the bouillon cube (if not using broth). Add the stuffed zucchini and reduce the heat to medium-high. Cook the zucchini for 15 to 20 minutes, or until easily pierced with a knife.

Remove the saucepan from the heat. Stir in the green onion and cilantro. Serve with Steamed Rice (page 61).

Egg Drop Soup

Canh Trứng

Canh trứng is a simple soup served as an appetizer or with rice. This Vietnamese version of egg drop soup is slightly different from the Chinese version, which has a thicker broth. Generally, there are no tomatoes or fish sauce in the Chinese version. With these additions, the soup acquires a subtle sweet-and-sour flavor.

1 tablespoon vegetable oil

4 ounces ground pork, beef, chicken, or turkey

¼ cup finely chopped onion

2 medium-size tomatoes, cut into wedges

2 tablespoons fish sauce

1 cube chicken-flavored bouillon

½ teaspoon salt

1 egg, lightly beaten

¼ cup finely chopped green onion

¼ cup finely chopped fresh cilantro

⅛ teaspoon black pepper

Heat the oil in a medium-size nonstick saucepan over medium-high heat. Cook the meat and onion for 4 minutes or until the meat is no longer pink. Add 6 cups of water and bring to a boil. Stir in the tomato, fish sauce, bouillon cube, and salt. Cook for 5 minutes.

While stirring, slowly add the egg. (Stirring helps prevent the egg from clumping together.) Cook for 3 more minutes.

Remove the saucepan from the heat. Add the green onion, cilantro, and black pepper. Serve with Steamed Rice (page 61) or as an appetizer.

Variation: For tofu lovers, ½ (4-ounce) package diced firm tofu may be added to the soup just before the egg.

Tofu Egg Drop Soup

Canh Đậu Hủ Với Trứng

2 to 4 servings

Canh đậu hủ với trứng *includes tofu, tomatoes, onion, and seasonings in a chicken broth. The tofu absorbs the flavor of the broth and takes on a hearty taste. Many meat dishes go well with tofu soup.*

¼ (4-ounce) package firm tofu

1 tablespoon vegetable oil

2 tablespoons finely chopped onion

2 medium-size tomatoes, cut into wedges

1 cube chicken-flavored bouillon or 1 cup chicken broth

1 teaspoon fish sauce

½ teaspoon salt

1 egg, lightly beaten

¼ cup finely chopped green onion

¼ cup finely chopped fresh cilantro

⅛ teaspoon black pepper

Dice the tofu into ½-inch cubes. Heat the oil in a saucepan over medium-high heat for 1 to 2 minutes. Add the onion and sauté until golden brown. Add the tomato and stir for 1 minute. Pour 4 cups of water (3 cups if using broth) and the broth over the vegetables. Add the bouillon cube, fish sauce, and salt. Bring to a boil.

Add the tofu and, stirring occasionally, return the broth to a boil. While stirring slowly add the egg. (Stirring helps to prevent the egg from clumping.) Cook for 3 more minutes, stirring occasionally. Remove from the heat. Add the green onion, cilantro, and black pepper. Serve with Steamed Rice (page 61) or as an appetizer.

nd-Sour Soup

4 servings

1 pound catfish, cleaned

1 cup vegetable oil

1 medium-size onion, finely chopped

5 teaspoons tamarind powder

¼ cup crushed and drained pineapple

2 tablespoons fish sauce

1 teaspoon salt

2 teaspoons sugar

1 cube chicken bouillon

4 ounces fresh okra, trimmed and halved lengthwise

2 tomatoes, cut into wedges

¼ pound bean sprouts

2 tara stems (bạc hà), peeled and sliced diagonally ½ to 1 inch thick (optional)

¼ cup finely chopped green onion

⅛ teaspoon black pepper

1 package rau ôm mint leaves, finely chopped (optional)

1 Thai red pepper, minced (optional)

The head and tail of a catfish are traditionally served in this soup, while the remainder of the cooked fish is used for other dishes, such as Catfish Pepper Stew (page 116). Using an entire fish may seem strange, but this soup is a Vietnamese favorite. Besides, nothing goes to waste when Bác Kít cooks. However, if you are squeamish, you may omit the head and tail.

Cut the fish into 2-inch lengths.

Heat the oil in a frying pan over medium-high heat. Fry the fish for 5 minutes on each side, or until lightly golden on both sides. This helps to reduce the fishy flavor. (Note: The fish should not be well done at this point, or it will overcook in the soup.) Drain the oil and set the fish aside.

Pour 6 cups of water into a large saucepan with the onion, tamarind powder, pineapple, fish sauce, salt, and sugar. Bring to a boil over medium-high heat, then add the fish. Cook for 30 minutes over medium heat. Add the bouillon cube, okra, and tomato, and return to a boil. Add the bean sprouts and tara stems, and return to a boil.

Remove the saucepan from the heat. Add the green onion and black pepper, along with the desired amount of mint and pepper.

Pickled Green Fish-Head Soup

Canh Dưa Chua Đàu Cá

2 to 4 servings

Don't be alarmed—the taste is better than the name, but it sure gets your attention! Canh dưa chua đàu cá *features a fish head and tail. You may, however, substitute any other fish parts. The main reason for the head and tail is to utilize every part of the fish. Since the head consists mostly of bones, and bones contain marrow, the fish head makes great broth. The rest of the fish may be used for other recipes such as Catfish Pepper Stew (page 116) or Sautéed Catfish (page 139). Other firm fish, such as perch, also work well in this recipe.*

1 pound catfish cleaned and cut in 1- to 2-inch pieces

1½ cups vegetable oil

½ cup finely chopped onion

2 tomatoes, cut into wedges

3 cups drained pickled mustard greens (dưa chua) *(page 26)*

2 tablespoons fish sauce

1 teaspoon sugar

1 teaspoon salt

⅛ teaspoon black pepper

¼ cup finely chopped green onion

Heat the oil in a large frying pan for 2 to 3 minutes over medium-high heat. (Warning: Be sure to dry the fish to help prevent splattering.) Place the fish in the pan and cover. Fry on both sides for 5 minutes each, or until golden brown. Transfer to a dish, reserving 1 tablespoon of the oil in the pan.

Heat the reserved oil in the pan for 1 to 2 minutes over medium-high heat. Sauté the onion until golden brown. Add the tomato, pickled greens, fish sauce, sugar, and salt. Cook for 10 minutes. Add 5 cups of water and bring to a boil. Add the fish and cook for 10 minutes.

Remove the saucepan from the heat. Mix the green onion and black pepper into the soup. Serve with Steamed Rice (page 61).

Asparagus Crab Soup

Súp Măng Cua

4 servings

Traditionally, súp măng cua *is served on special occasions, such as weddings or Giổ. Imitation crabmeat, which is composed primarily of pollock, is used instead of genuine crab as it is less expensive. If you prefer the exotic flavor of real crabmeat, it may be substituted. Vietnamese restaurants serve this soup as an appetizer.*

4 ounces boneless chicken

1 (8-ounce) can chicken broth

2 ounces imitation crab, shredded

2 chicken-flavored bouillon cubes

2 ounces drained straw mushrooms, halved

½ teaspoon salt

4 ounces fresh asparagus, tops discarded, chopped into ¼-inch lengths

2 tablespoons cornstarch

1 egg, lightly beaten

¼ cup finely chopped fresh cilantro

⅛ teaspoon black pepper

Place the chicken in a large saucepan with 6 cups of water. Bring to a boil over high heat, then reduce the heat to medium. Cook for 20 minutes. Reduce the heat to low and simmer for an additional 40 minutes. Remove the chicken from the pot and add the broth to the cooking liquid. Use your fingers to shred the chicken into bite-size pieces and set aside.

Add the imitation crab, half the chicken, the bouillon cubes, mushrooms, and salt to the broth. Bring to a boil over medium-high heat, stirring occasionally. Add the asparagus and return to a boil.

While waiting for the broth to boil, mix the cornstarch with ¼ cup of water in a small bowl. Once the broth is boiling, slowly stir in the cornstarch mixture, then slowly stir in the egg. Stir constantly to prevent clumping, and return to a boil.

Remove the saucepan from the heat. Sprinkle with the cilantro and black pepper.

A Vietnamese Kitchen

Salad with Lemon Dressing

Xà Lách Trộn Chanh

Xà lách trộn chanh *is a light, lemony salad and may be served with such dishes as Roasted Chicken (page 125) and Lemon Pepper Chicken (page 122).*

---

1 medium-size head iceberg or romaine lettuce, chopped

1 tablespoon lemon juice

2½ teaspoons sugar

½ teaspoon salt

1 teaspoon vegetable oil

½ onion, thinly sliced

1 tomato, thinly sliced

½ cup (2 1/4 ounces) finely chopped unsalted roasted peanuts

Mix the lemon juice, sugar, and salt in a small bowl. In a large salad bowl, toss the lettuce with the oil, onion, tomato, and peanuts. Add two-thirds of the lemon juice mixture to the salad and mix well. Taste the salad and add additional lemon dressing as desired. Serve as an appetizer or a side dish.

Lemon Chicken Salad

Gà ướp Chanh   2 *servings*

Bác Kít invented this tasty yet simple salad that uses leftover chicken. Seafood, other meats or poultry, such as leftover turkey from Thanksgiving, works wonderfully in this salad as well.

---

1 pound boneless and skinless chicken, any parts

¼ cup finely chopped green onion

¼ cup finely chopped fresh cilantro

1 teaspoon finely chopped fresh ginger

½ teaspoon salt

1½ tablespoons lemon juice

1 tablespoon sugar

¼ teaspoon black pepper

¼ teaspoon pepper sauce or hot chili sauce (tương ớt) (optional)

5 lemon leaves, finely chopped (optional)

½ teaspoon finely chopped chili pepper (optional)

Place the chicken in a saucepan with water to cover. Bring to a boil over high heat, then reduce the heat to medium. Cook for 30 minutes, or until the chicken is cooked through. Remove the saucepan from the heat. Drain the broth and reserve it for a future use.

Shred the chicken into bite-size pieces. Combine the chicken, green onion, cilantro, ginger, salt, lemon juice, sugar, and black pepper. Mix well. Add the pepper sauce, lemon leaves, and chili pepper.

Serve with Steamed Rice (page 61), bread, or as an appetizer with crackers.

Tip: Nothing goes to waste. The chicken broth may be used in such dishes as Asparagus Crab Soup (page 52) or Glass Noodle Chicken Soup (page 70).

A Vietnamese Kitchen

Vietnamese Chicken Coleslaw

Gỏi Gà

Gỏi gà *is a Vietnamese-style coleslaw. It is generally served with* cháo gà *(page 69) as a light meal. Traditionally, this dish is prepared for special occasions such as* Giỗ *or* Tết.

1 boneless and skinless chicken breast

1 head cabbage, shredded

1 carrot, peeled and shredded

3 tablespoons lemon juice

2 teaspoons sugar

1 teaspoon salt

¼ teaspoon black pepper

1 tablespoon finely chopped green onion

¼ cup (1¼ ounces) finely chopped unsalted peanuts

½ small onion, thinly sliced

½ cup finely chopped fresh cilantro

½ cup finely chopped rau răm *mint (optional)*

Place the chicken breast in a saucepan with enough water to cover. Bring to a boil over high heat, then reduce the heat to medium-high. Cook until the chicken is cooked through, 15 to 20 minutes. Drain the broth from the chicken, reserving it for a future use. Shred the chicken into bite-size pieces.

In a large bowl, combine the cabbage and carrot. Mix the lemon juice, sugar, salt, black pepper, and green onion in a small bowl. Pour the lemon mixture over the cabbage and carrots. Add the shredded chicken, peanuts, onion, cilantro, and mint. Mix well.

Tip: For an extra zing, try adding in Spicy Lemon Fish Sauce (page 22).

Saigon Beef Salad

Thịt Bò Lúc Lắc

Thịt bò lúc lắc originated in southern Vietnam. This stir-fry is a mixture of diced tender beef, potatoes, tomatoes, and onions in a delightful sauce. It is served on a bed of lettuce.

½ pound beef sirloin or any tender cut of beef, diced into ½-inch cubes

1 tablespoon oyster sauce

2 tablespoons soy sauce

2 tablespoons finely chopped onions

1 teaspoon minced garlic

2 medium-size potatoes, cooked and chilled

1 cup vegetable oil

2 teaspoons lemon juice

2 teaspoons sugar

¼ teaspoon salt

2 medium-size tomatoes, seeded and diced

1 tablespoon prepared mustard

⅛ teaspoon black pepper

1 medium-size head romaine or iceberg lettuce, chopped

In a bowl, combine the beef, oyster sauce, soy sauce, onion, and garlic. Mix well. Cover and refrigerate for 15 minutes.

Peel and dice the chilled potatoes into ½-inch cubes. Heat the oil in a large frying pan for 1 to 2 minutes over medium-high heat. Fry the potatoes until golden brown. Transfer to a bowl lined with paper towels to absorb excess oil, reserving 1 tablespoon of oil in the pan.

Heat the reserved oil in the pan over high heat. Add the beef mixture and stir for 2 minutes. Add the tomatoes and potatoes, and stir for 1 minute. Add the mustard and mix well. Remove the frying pan from the heat. Sprinkle the black pepper over the beef.

In a bowl, combine the lemon juice, sugar, and salt. Toss the lettuce with the lemon juice mixture. Divide the salad into 4 portions. Top each salad with the beef.

Serve as an appetizer or with rice.

Lemon Beef Salad

Thịt Bò Xào Chanh

2 servings

Thịt bò xào chanh is served as a side dish, with soup, or with Steamed Rice (page 61). This dish is not a traditional everyday dish, but a stir-fry with a French flare served in restaurants and on special occasions.

½ pound beef sirloin, thinly sliced

1 tablespoon soy sauce

1 tablespoon oyster sauce

2 teaspoons minced garlic

⅛ teaspoon black pepper

3 teaspoons vegetable oil

1 onion, finely chopped

2 tablespoons lemon juice

1 tablespoon sugar

1 teaspoon salt

1 medium-size head romaine or iceberg lettuce, chopped

¼ cup finely chopped fresh cilantro

2 medium-size tomatoes, thinly sliced

½ cup (2¼-ounce) finely chopped unsalted peanuts

In a bowl, combine the beef with the soy sauce, oyster sauce, garlic, and black pepper. Cover and refrigerate for at least 15 minutes.

Heat 2 teaspoons of the oil in a large frying pan or wok. Add 2 teaspoons of the chopped onion. Stir until golden brown. Remove the pan from the heat.

In a small bowl, mix the lemon juice with the sugar and salt. In a large bowl, toss the lettuce with the fried onion, lemon juice mixture, remaining onion, and cilantro.

Heat the remaining 1 teaspoon of oil in the pan. Add the marinated beef and stir for 5 [m]in-utes, or until the desired doneness is achiev[ed]. Remove the frying pan from the heat.

Arrange the tomato over the salad. Place th[e] cooked beef on top of the tomato. Sprinkle [with] the peanuts.

Serve with soup or as an appetizer.

Rice and Noodles

Rice has been a staple for generations of Vietnamese. It is served at every meal, packed tightly in a small bowl. Other foods, such as soup, stir-fries, or *kho*, are placed on top. Without rice, there would not be enough soup, stir-fry, or *kho* to go around. (The average Vietnamese family includes six to eight members at all times. It is not uncommon for two or three different families, including the in-laws and their children, to live in one household.) Rice is cheap and abundant, hence it serves as the perennial extender in Vietnamese meals.

I had to learn to appreciate the grain. To a child, having it every day was boring. I found plenty of excuses to avoid eating it. As I grew older, though, the positive qualities of rice grew on me and now I am attached to it—my meal is unfulfilling if it is absent.

There are many types of rice. Rice farmers strive continuously to improve its texture, color, and fragrance. The varieties usually used in Vietnamese cooking are regular white long-grain rice, jasmine rice, and sweet (sticky) rice. Jasmine rice is the most popular kind eaten by Vietnamese Americans. Buddha, Three Ladies, and Flying Goose are a few brand names to look for. My husband claims that the freshly cooked jasmine rice has the same aroma as freshly popped popcorn. As for white and sweet rice, every brand is a little different; sample several to see which you prefer. The four-digit number on the package refers to the year the rice was grown. As with vintages of wine, the environmental conditions of a particular year affect the grain.

Noodles are the secondary staple food in Vietnam. They are eaten most frequently in the north where wheat is more prevalent than rice. There are many kinds of noodles, each with its own shape, flavor, color, and texture. Some are made of rice flour, others from mung beans, or wheat. This cookbook uses such rice noodles as *bún* and *phở*. *Bún* noodles are thin, round, threadlike strands also known as rice sticks or rice vermicelli. *Phở* noodles are flat and wide. *Miến* noodles, also known as glass or bean thread noodles, are made from mung beans. Thin and round, they are similar to *bún* but are transparent instead of white. Wheat-based egg noodles are yellow and called *mì*. Whichever kind you prefer, noodles are a great substitute for rice when you want a change of pace.

Each recipe, except for Steamed Rice, Steamed Broken Rice, and Boiled Dry Noodles, in this chapter could be categorized as stand alone meal. The primary difference between the soups in this chapter versus the soups in the Soup and Salad chapter (page 41) is the presence of noodles. With the noodles as part of the soup, the Vietnamese consider it as a substantial meal.

Often, I prepare noodle soups in large quantities. There are three primary reasons for this. First, it takes the same amount of time, at nearly the same minimal cost, to prepare enough soup for four or twelve. Secondly, you can also easily freeze the leftovers. It is never too much. Thirdly, it is simply force of habit: I grew up in a family of ten—everything was prepared in bulk. I find it economical and efficient to make noodle dishes when I need to feed a large number of friends or relatives.

Steamed Rice

Cơm

Steamed rice can be prepared in a rice cooker or a regular saucepan. Because the heat is not distributed evenly in a saucepan, however, the rice burns more easily. Using a rice cooker, which has a thermostat, is the preferred method.

4 cups rice (gạo) (such as Buddha-brand jasmine rice)

Rice Cooker Instructions:

Rinse the uncooked rice in the rice cooker's steamer container until the water becomes clear. Drain. Add 3½ cups of water to the rice. Place the container in the cooker and press the "cook" button. Allow the rice to cook until the button pops up. The cooker is usually kept plugged in to keep the cooked rice warm. As rice cookers age they will eventually burn the rice on the bottom. Unplugging the cooker to stop the cooking process when the rice is done is one way to prevent rice from burning. This will take approximately 15 minutes. Fluff the rice with a large spoon, chopsticks, or a fork.

Stovetop Instructions:

Rinse the rice in the saucepan until the water becomes clear. Drain. Add 4 cups of water to the rice. Cover and cook for 3 to 5 minutes over medium-high heat, or until the water boils. Uncover and stir once. Reduce the heat to medium-low. Cover and cook for 2 minutes. Uncover and stir once more. Reduce the heat to low and cook, covered, for 2 minutes. Reduce the heat to as low as possible. Cover and cook for 10 more minutes, or until the rice grains are soft and fluffy. Remove the saucepan from the heat. Fluff the rice with a large spoon, chopsticks, or a fork.

Tips: The proportion of water and rice may differ, depending on the brand. A traditional method of measuring the water is by using the index finger as a measuring device. The water level should be up to the first joint of the index finger, measuring from the top of the uncooked rice. You would think that this method is not accurate because everyone has different finger size, but somehow it always works. This method has been passed down through generations of my family. Now, I am passing it on to you.

Steamed Broken Rice

Cơm Tấm

Milled or white rice is the rice most commonly eaten in Vietnam. In the milling process, the husks and bran are removed, leaving only the core, which is starch. The grains that break during the milling process are sold separately as broken rice, which may be found in many Asian stores. It has a drier texture than whole-grain rice.

Cơm tấm is often served with grilled pork and Sweet-and-Sour Fish Sauce (page 23) during special festivities. In Vietnam, street vendors serve it with meat, seafood, or vegetables for breakfast, lunch, and dinner.

Like regular rice, cơm tấm *can be prepared in a rice cooker or in a saucepan. Because heat is not distributed evenly on the stovetop, rice burns more easily. The preparation for* cơm tấm *is slightly different than that for regular steamed rice. Please read the instructions completely before preparing.*

---

3 cups uncooked broken rice (gạo tấm)

1½ cups young coconut juice (nước dừa)

Rice Cooker Instructions:

Place the rice in the rice cooker's steamer container with enough hot water to cover. Soak for 30 minutes. Rinse until the water becomes clear. Drain. Add 1½ cups of water and the coconut juice. Place the container in the cooker and press the "cook" button. Cook until the button pops up approximately 15 minutes. Fluff the cooked rice with a large spoon, chopsticks, or a fork.

Stovetop Instructions:

Place the rice in a bowl with enough hot water to cover. Soak for 30 minutes. Rinse until the water becomes clear. Drain. Pour 1½ cups of water and the coconut juice into a saucepan. Bring to a boil over medium-high heat. Add the broken-rice. Cover and cook for 3 to 5 minutes, or until the water boils. Uncover and stir once. Reduce the heat to medium-low, cover, and cook for 2 minutes. Uncover and stir once more. Reduce the heat to low, cover, and cook for 2 minutes. Reduce the heat to as low as possible, and cover and cook for 10 more minutes, or until the rice grains are soft and fluffy, and not too dry or mushy. Fluff the rice with a large spoon, chopsticks, or a fork. Remove the saucepan from the heat.

Tip: Similar to regular rice, the proportion of water, coconut juice, and rice may differ by brand. Use your own judgment and preference for the proportion between the water and coconut juice. Broken rice is difficult to perfect at first try, so don't be discouraged. Experimentation is the key to success.

Boiled Dried Noodles

Luộc Bún Khô hay Phở Khô   *4 to 6 servings*

Certain noodles require longer cooking than others. There are dried, uncooked noodles and fresh, cooked noodles. Dried uncooked noodles, such as bún (vermicelli rice sticks) and phở noodles, require boiling for five to ten minutes. Miến (bean thread) noodles are also sold dried, but are easily overcooked. Soaking miến noodles in hot water before cooking prevents them from expanding and absorbing too much water. Hard-to-find fresh, cooked noodles require boiling for only two to three minutes, just enough to warm them.

This recipe provides basic instructions for boiling dried Asian noodles, which are a component of many dishes in this book.

---

*16 ounces dried noodles
(bún or phở)*

Bring 8 cups of water to a boil in a large saucepan. Gradually add the noodles to the water so that the water continues to boil. Keep the saucepan uncovered and stir occasionally until the noodles are tender, 5 to 10 minutes, or as directed on the package.

Remove the saucepan from the heat. Immediately drain the noodles in a colander or sieve. Run cold water over them for a few minutes and drain. The cold water prevents the noodles from sticking together.

Egg Fried Rice

Cơm Chiên Trứng

Cơm chiên trứng is the simplest form of fried rice and leftover steamed rice is great for this dish. Occasionally I am too tired or too lazy to cook, egg fried rice is my fall back dish because it is quick, easy, and tasty.

1 recipe Steamed Rice (page 61), warm

2 teaspoons seasoning salt (such as Lawry's)

3 eggs

¼ cup finely chopped green onion

4 teaspoons soy sauce

2 tablespoons vegetable oil

¼ cup finely chopped onion

½ teaspoon mushroom seasoning (optional)

⅛ teaspoon black pepper

Mix the cooked rice and seasoning salt in a large bowl. Allow the rice to cool for 5 to 10 minutes. Combine the eggs, green onion, and soy sauce.

Heat the oil in a frying pan over medium-high heat. Add the onion to the oil and stir until golden brown. Add the steamed rice and cook, stirring, for 5 minutes. Slowly stir the egg mixture into the rice and cook, stirring, for 3 minutes. Add the mushroom seasoning. Reduce the heat to low and cook, stirring, for 3 more minutes.

Remove the frying pan from the heat. Sprinkle black pepper on top.

Tip: Keep in mind that refrigerated cooked rice needs to be reheated before use. One quick way to do this, is to sprinkle 1 teaspoon of water over the rice and microwave it on HIGH for 30 seconds or until the rice softens.

Sizzling Combo Fried Rice

Cơm Chiên Thập Cẩm

Cơm chiên thập cẩm *is elaborate and suitable for special occasions. You may add other meats or seafood such as shrimp to this dish.*

The mushroom seasoning is an MSG substitute and an optional ingredient. I would recommend adding the mushroom seasoning to this dish if you have it. It will definitely enhance the flavor of the fried rice.

---

2 cups mixed vegetables (such as green peas and carrots)

4 ounces ground meat any kind

1 teaspoon oyster sauce

½ cup finely chopped onion

1 recipe Steamed Rice (page 61)

3 teaspoons seasoning salt (such as Lawry's)

2 eggs, lightly beaten

5 teaspoons vegetable oil

3 tablespoons soy sauce

½ teaspoon mushroom seasoning (optional)

⅛ teaspoon black pepper

Place the mixed vegetables in a saucepan with 4 cups of water. Bring to a boil over high heat. Remove the saucepan from the heat. Drain the vegetables thoroughly for 10 to 15 minutes in a strainer.

Meanwhile, combine the meat with the oyster sauce and 1 tablespoon of the onion. Cover and refrigerate for 15 minutes.

Allow the steamed rice to cool for 5 to 10 minutes. (Cooling the rice prevents it from becoming mushy.) Stir 2 teaspoons of the seasoning salt into the rice. In a bowl, mix the vegetables with the remaining 1 teaspoon of seasoning salt.

Heat a nonstick frying pan over medium-high heat. Add the meat and cook, stirring, for 3 minutes. Add the mixed vegetables, and cook, stirring, for 2 minutes. Transfer the meat and vegetables to a bowl.

Heat 1 teaspoon of the oil in the same frying pan for 1 minute over medium-high heat. Pour in 1 tablespoon of the egg mixture. Quickly tilt the frying pan to spread the mixture thinly until it covers the pan bottom. Cook until the egg solidifies. Transfer the egg crepe to a dish. Make 2 to 3 egg crepes. Finely chop each crepe.

Heat the remaining 4 teaspoons of oil in the same frying pan over medium-high heat for 30 seconds to 1 minute. Add the remaining onion and cook, stirring, until lightly golden brown. Add the rice and cook, stirring, for 5 minutes. Slowly, stir in the meat, vegetables, soy sauce, and mushroom seasoning, and cook, stirring for 10 more minutes.

Remove the frying pan from the heat. Mix in the egg crepe. Sprinkle black pepper on top of the rice.

Tips: Leftover cooked rice can be used for fried rice. Keep in mind, refrigerated rice needs to be reheated before use (see page 65).

The main secret to successful sizzling fried rice is cooking the vegetables, meat, and eggs separately. If you cook everything together, the rice absorbs the juices from the other ingredients and becomes mushy.

Veggie Fried Rice

Cơm Chiên với Đậu Hòa Lan

Cơm chiên với đậu Hòa Lan *is a vegetarian version of Sizzling Combo Fried Rice (page 66). Leftover steamed rice is ideal for this dish.*

2 cups mixed frozen and chopped vegetables (such as green peas and carrots)

1 recipe Steamed Rice (page 61), warm

1 tablespoon seasoning salt (such as Lawry's)

2 eggs

¼ cup finely chopped green onion

5 teaspoons vegetable oil

¼ cup finely chopped onion

3 tablespoons soy sauce

½ teaspoon mushroom seasoning (optional)

⅛ teaspoon black pepper

While the rice is cooking, place the mixed vegetables in a saucepan with 4 cups of water. Bring to a boil over high heat. Remove the saucepan from the heat. Drain the vegetables in a colander for 10 to 15 minutes.

After the rice is cooked, allow it to cool for 5 to 10 minutes. Mix the rice and 2 teaspoons of the seasoning salt in a large bowl. Mix the vegetables with the remaining 1 teaspoon of seasoning salt. Break the eggs into a small bowl and beat with the green onion.

Heat 1 teaspoon of the oil in a frying pan over medium-high heat. Add the mixed vegetables and cook, stirring, for 2 minutes. Transfer the vegetables to a bowl.

Heat the remaining 4 teaspoons of oil in the same frying pan over medium-high heat for 1 minute. Add the onion and stir until lightly golden brown. Add the steamed rice and cook, stirring, for 5 minutes. Slowly stir in the egg mixture and cook, stirring, for 3 minutes. Add the vegetables, soy sauce, and mushroom seasoning, and cook, stirring, for 5 more minutes or until everything is well mixed.

Remove the frying pan from the heat. Sprinkle black pepper on top.

Tips: Keep in mind, refrigerated cooked rice needs to be reheated before use (see page 65).

Chicken and Rice Soup

Cháo gà

Cháo gà is a rice gruel served for breakfast or lunch. It is light yet filling. Like chicken soup in the United States, it is used as a Vietnamese cold remedy. Many people believe that the warmth of the broth and the wholesomeness of the chicken help regain one's strength.

½ pound skinless, boneless chicken, any parts

2 (14-ounce) cans chicken broth

1 cup rice

3 cubes chicken-flavored bouillon

2 tablespoons fish sauce

¼ teaspoon salt

¼ cup finely chopped onion

1 tablespoon finely chopped fresh ginger

½ cup finely chopped fresh cilantro

½ cup finely chopped green onion

¼ teaspoon black pepper

½ pound bean sprouts

½ lemon, quartered

Place the chicken in a large saucepan with enough water to cover. Bring to a boil over high heat. Remove the saucepan from the heat and drain. (Boiling the chicken helps clean and reduce the excess fat from the chicken.)

Return the chicken to the saucepan. Add 10 cups of water and the broth, and bring to a boil over high heat. Then, reduce the heat to medium-low.

Rinse the uncooked rice at least once to clean it. Add the rice to the broth and simmer for 30 minutes.

If the soup becomes so thick that it is difficult to stir with a spoon, add 2 more cups of water. The final consistency should be similar to porridge or gruel. You do not want it to be too thick to stir, nor too runny. Remove the chicken and tear it into bite-size pieces. Set aside.

After 30 minutes, add the bouillon cubes, fish sauce, salt, onion, and chicken to the broth. Cook for 25 more minutes over low heat. Taste the broth and adjust the salt.

Remove the saucepan from the heat. Mix in the ginger, cilantro, green onion, and black pepper. Serve with a handful of bean sprouts and a squirt of lemon juice.

Tip: Most canned chicken broth contains MSG and high sodium content. Read the label carefully.

Glass Noodle Chicken Soup

Canh Miến Thịt Gà

Canh miến thịt gà *originates in northern Vietnam. A good companion dish is boiled chicken dipped in Spicy Lemon Fish Sauce (page 22).*

2 pounds chicken, any parts

4 (1.8-ounce) bundles bean thread noodles, (miến)

½ cup chopped dried black mushrooms

2 cubes chicken-flavored bouillon

1 teaspoon salt

2 tablespoons fish sauce

¼ cup finely chopped onion

½ cup finely chopped green onion

¼ cup finely chopped fresh cilantro

⅛ teaspoon black pepper

Clean the chicken thoroughly. If you are using chicken breasts, quarter them. Place the chicken in a large saucepan with 12 cups of water. Bring the water to a boil over high heat, then reduce the heat to medium-low. Simmer for another 50 minutes.

Meanwhile, soak the noodles and dried mushrooms in separate bowls of hot water for 10 minutes. Drain. Cut the noodles into 6-inch lengths.

After 50 minutes, skim the foam from the broth. Remove the chicken, tear it into bite-size pieces, and set aside. Add the mushrooms, bouillon cubes, salt, fish sauce, and onion to the broth. Cook for 10 minutes over medium heat. Taste the broth and adjust the seasoning with additional salt if necessary. Add half or all of the torn chicken pieces to the broth and remove the saucepan from the heat. Bác Kít suggests using half of the chicken for dishes such as Lemon Chicken Salad (page 54). This way you can have a soup and salad meal.

To avoid overcooking the noodles, return the broth to a boil 10 minutes before serving. Add the noodles and mix well. Cook for 3 minutes, then remove the saucepan from the heat. (Warning: *Miến* noodles expand and absorb the soup very quickly if overcooked or are allowed to sit for more than 10 minutes.) Add the green onion, cilantro, and black pepper to the soup.

Serve with Steamed Rice (page 61) and boiled chicken or as an appetizer. This soup tastes best when served hot.

Vietnamese Chicken Noodle Soup

Phở Gà

4 servings

Phở gà is similar to phở bò, *however, the noodles are cooked in chicken broth instead of beef broth. Mint leaves, bean sprouts, hoisin sauce, lemon, and hot chili peppers are the traditional accompaniments.*

1 (2-pound) chicken

1-inch piece fresh ginger, halved

1 medium-size onion, halved

3 cubes chicken-flavored phở *bouillon*

1 (1-ounce) bag gia vị nấu phở *(phở flavor)**

1 teaspoon sugar

1 teaspoon salt

1 (16-ounce) package phở *noodles, cooked (page 64)*

½ lemon, quartered

½ cup finely chopped green onions

½ cup finely chopped fresh cilantro

½ pound bean sprouts

1 bunch basil

Hoisin sauce (optional)

Red Thai peppers, chili, or pepper sauce (optional)

Wash the chicken, remove the neck and giblets, and quarter it. Place the chicken in a 4-quart saucepan with water to cover and bring to a boil over high heat. Remove the saucepan from the heat and drain. This helps clean the chicken and reduces excess fat. Return the chicken to the same saucepan with 3½ quarts of water. Bring to a boil over high heat.

Meanwhile toast the ginger and onion over an open flame or burner. The ginger and onion should be in direct contact with the flame. Constantly rotate to toast all sides until crisp. This will add a subtle burnt flavor to the soup. If you do not have a gas stove, toast the ginger and onion in a dry skillet until browned. Rinse and drain the ginger and onion. Thinly slice the ginger. Add the onion and ginger to the broth. Once boiling, reduce the heat to medium-low. Simmer for 30 minutes.

Add the *phở* bouillon, *gia vị nấu phở*, sugar, and salt to the broth. Reduce the heat to low and simmer for 30 minutes. Remove only the chicken breasts from the broth, shred them into bite-size pieces, and set aside.

After 30 minutes, taste the broth and adjust with additional salt if necessary. Remove the remaining chicken pieces, *gia vị nấu phở*, ginger, and onion, leaving only the broth. Skim any foam from the broth. Tear the remaining chicken into bite-size pieces.

Divide the *phở* noodles between four bowls. Place the chicken on top, and pour in the broth. Add a squirt of lemon juice, green onions, cilantro, bean sprouts, and basil to each bowl. Add hoisin sauce and peppers according to each person's preference. These condiments are usually added by each diner at the table.

*If *gia vị nấu phở* is not available, toast 1 tablespoon aniseed, 10 whole cloves, and ½ cinnamon stick in a dry skillet over medium heat. Place the spices in cheese-cloth and tie with kitchen twine. If you cannot find *phở* bouillon cubes, use beef-flavored bouillon cubes and 2 teaspoons mushroom seasoning (optional).

Vietnamese Beef Noodle Soup
Phở Bò

4 servings

Phở bò—rice noodles and thinly sliced beef served in beef broth—is the most popular Vietnamese dish. It is one of my family's favorite noodle soups. Knowing our weakness for phở, *my parents bribed all the children including myself with an unlimited amount of* phở *once we arrived in America, in return for our promise to behave and cooperate. It worked.*

Most Vietnamese eat phở *for breakfast; however, it is also good for lunch, dinner, or a midnight snack. It is served with mint leaves, bean sprouts, hoisin sauce, lemon, and hot peppers.*

Place the oxtails in a 4-quart saucepan with water to cover. Bring to a boil over high heat and remove the saucepan from the heat. Drain. This helps clean the meat and reduces excess fat. Return the oxtails to the same saucepan with 4 quarts of water. Bring to a boil over high heat.

Meanwhile toast them over an open flame or burner. The ginger and onion should be in direct contact with the flame. Constantly rotate to toast all the sides. This adds a subtle burnt flavor to the soup. If you do not have a gas stove, toast the ginger and onion in a dry skillet until browned. Rinse and drain the roasted ginger and onion. Thinly slice the ginger. Add the onion and ginger to the broth. Once boiling, reduce the heat to medium-low, cover and simmer for 1 hour.

Add the bouillon cubes, *gia vị nấu phở*, sugar, and salt to the broth. Cook for 40 minutes. Taste the broth and adjust with additional salt if necessary. Remove the oxtail, ginger, *gia vị nấu phở*, and onion. Reserve the broth. Reduce the heat to low, and skim any foam off the broth.

3 pounds oxtails, chopped into 1- to 2-inch pieces

1-inch piece fresh ginger, halved

1 medium-size onion, halved

4 cubes beef-flavored phở *bouillon*

1 (1-ounce) bag gia vị nấu phở (phở flavor)*

1 teaspoon sugar

1 teaspoon salt

1 (16-ounce) package phở *noodles, cooked (page 64)*

1 pound beef sirloin, thinly sliced

½ lemon, quartered

½ cup finely chopped green onion

½ cup finely chopped fresh cilantro

½ pound bean sprouts

1 bunch Thai basil (húng phở), stemmed

Thai red peppers, chili, or pepper sauce (optional)

Hoisin sauce (optional)

Divide the *phở* noodles among four bowls. Spread 10 to 12 pieces of raw beef over the noodles. Pour in the hot broth, which will cook the beef to medium-rare. If a diner prefers well-done beef, place the beef in a soup ladle and dip the ladle into the simmering broth, to cook the beef to the desired doneness.

Add a few squirts of lemon juice to each bowl. Mix in green onions, cilantro, bean sprouts, basil, peppers, and hoisin sauce according to each person's preference.

*See page 73.

Huế-Style Beef Noodle Soup

Bún Bò Huế

Bún bò Huế is a hot and spicy specialty that originated in central Vietnam. The authentic version of this treat will leave you sitting in a puddle of sweat. Bác Kít's recipe, however, reduces the amount of spiciness by tenfold. But if you want it hot and spicy, add more peppers.

Generally, this soup is very greasy and filled with plenty of fatty meats such as pork fat. However, Bác Kít reduced the amount of fat in this tasty soup. I have included a second method to prepare this recipe using exotic dried shrimp sauce, mắm tôm.

Rinse the meat under cold water and place it in a large pot with water to cover. Bring to a boil, then remove the pot from the heat. Drain. This helps clean the meat and reduces excess fat. Remove the tendons and fat from the beef and chop the tendons and fat into smaller pieces. Recombine with the rest of the meat.

In a large bowl, combine the meat with the onion, lemongrass, fish sauce, chili powder, bouillon cubes, garlic, black pepper and dried shrimp sauce. Mix well. Cover and refrigerate for at least 3 hours.

Place the meat and its juices in the large pot. Cook, stirring for 5 minutes over medium-high heat. Add 3¾ quarts of water and bring to a boil, then reduce the heat to medium. Cook for 1 hour.

Transfer the beef to a bowl. Cover and refrigerate. Pour 5 more cups of water into the pot. Increase the heat to high. Bring to a boil, then reduce the heat to low. Cook for 1 more hour. Taste the broth and adjust the seasoning with additional salt or water if necessary. Transfer the remaining pork from the broth to a bowl. Thinly slice the beef.

- *1 pound pork feet, each cut into 2 or 3 pieces*
- *1 pound pork hocks, cut into 2-inch pieces*
- *1 pound shank beef, cut into 2-inch pieces*
- *1 medium-size onion, cut into 12 wedges*
- *2 stalks lemongrass, finely chopped*
- *3 tablespoons fish sauce*
- *1 tablespoon* gia vị bún bò huế *chili powder**
- *3 cubes* bún bò huế-*flavor bouillon*
- *1 teaspoon finely chopped garlic*
- *⅛ teaspoon black pepper*
- *1 tablespoon dried shrimp sauce (*mắm tôm*) (optional)*
- *1½ (16-ounce) packages* bún bò huế *noodles, cooked; or 1½ (16-ounce) packages rice stick noodles (*bún*), cooked (page 64)*
- *½ cup finely chopped green onion*
- *½ pound bean sprouts*
- *1 bunch basil, stemmed*
- *1 lemon, sliced into 6 wedges*

Divide the noodles between six serving bowls. Place the beef slices on top of the noodles and pour in the broth. For you daredevils, add the pork feet and/or hocks to the soup bowls.

Serve with green onions, bean sprouts, and basil. Add a few squirts of lemon juice to each soup bowl.

Variation: This version of *bún bò huế* is traditional and a little lengthy but well worth the time if you love dried shrimp sauce. The night before, combine ¼ cup dried shrimp sauce and 3 cups of water in a bowl. Refrigerate the mixture overnight. All the solids will settle to the bottom of the bowl. When ready to cook, discard the sediment and reserve the water. Prepare according to the directions above, omitting the fish sauce and reducing the water to 17 cups total. Add the shrimp soaking water when you add the tablespoon of bottled shrimp sauce.

*If *gia vị bún bò huế* is not available, use 1 teaspoon chili powder, 1 teaspoon paprika, ½ teaspoon powdered ginger, and ½ teaspoon powdered onion.

Rice and Noodles

Rice Grilled Pork

Cơm Thịt Nướng   *4 servings*

Cơm thịt nướng *is similar to Grilled Pork Noodles (page 80). This dish can be served over steamed rice (page 61) or steamed broken rice (page 62). It is a popular dish because meat is a luxury ingredient for the average household in Vietnam. Because it is such a favorite at home, it is also on the menu of many Vietnamese restaurants.*

There are three different ways to cook the meat for cơm thịt nướng. *Each way has a different name in Vietnamese. Grilled meat is called* thịt nướng vỉ, *baked meat is called* thịt nướng lò hầm, *fried meat is called* thịt ram. *This recipe details the frying method. This recipe can be made with beef, chicken, turkey, or pork ribs.*

Slice the pork into ½ x 3-inch strips. Pound with a meat tenderizer. Combine the pork with the soy sauce, fish sauce, oyster sauce, hoisin sauce, black pepper, garlic, and onion in a bowl. Cover and refrigerate for at least 3 hours.

Combine the carrot, radish, lemon juice, sugar, salt, and chili and marinate for 1 to 3 hours in the refrigerator.

Heat 1 tablespoon of the oil in a frying pan over medium-high heat for 1 to 2 minutes. Cook the pork in a frying pan in a single layer, turning occasionally, until golden brown on both sides. Transfer to a serving plate and thinly slice the grilled pork.

Pour the remaining tablespoon of oil into the same frying pan. Add the green onions. Stir for 30 seconds. Remove the frying pan from the heat. Transfer the green onions to a small bowl.

2 pounds pork sirloin or
   boneless shoulder

2 tablespoons soy sauce

2 tablespoons fish sauce

2 tablespoons oyster sauce

1 tablespoon hoisin sauce

⅛ teaspoon black pepper

1 tablespoon finely
   chopped garlic

2 tablespoons finely
   chopped onion

1 cup peeled and grated
   carrot

1 cup peeled and shredded
   radish

1 tablespoon lemon juice

1 tablespoon sugar

½ teaspoon salt

⅛ teaspoon red chili

2 tablespoons vegetable oil

½ cup finely chopped
   green onion

1 cup peeled and shredded
   cucumber

1 recipe Steamed Rice
   (page 61) or Steamed
   Broken Rice (page 62)

2 cups Sweet-and-Sour
   Fish Sauce (page 23)

Thinly spread one quarter of the rice on four serving plates. Layer one quarter of the green onions and then one quarter of meat over the rice. Place the cucumbers and pickled vegetables on top of the meat. Pour 3 tablespoons or the desired amount of Sweet-and-Sour Fish Sauce over everything.

Tips: The meat can also be baked in an oven or barbecued shish kebab–style:
Baking: Preheat the oven to 350°F. Spread the meat on a baking sheet. Bake for approximately 25 minutes, or until golden brown.
Barbecuing: Skewer meat onto ten shish kebab sticks. Grill the meat on a barbecue grill for approximately 15 minutes, or until golden brown.

Rice and Noodles

Grilled Pork Noodles

Bún Thịt Nướng   *4 to 6 servings*

Bún thịt nướng is a simple, but popular dried noodle dish. This is one of my husband's favorites because the crispy, tender pork is well complemented by Sweet-and-Sour Fish Sauce (page 23). Egg rolls are a great substitute for grilled pork.

---

2 pounds pork sirloin or boneless shoulder

2 tablespoons soy sauce

2 tablespoons fish sauce

2 tablespoons oyster sauce

1 tablespoon hoisin sauce

1 tablespoon finely minced garlic

2 tablespoons chopped onion

½ cup finely chopped green onion

½ cup finely chopped lemongrass

⅛ teaspoon black pepper

1 (16-ounce) package rice stick noodles (bún), cooked (page 64)

1 bunch mint, stemmed

1 bunch cilantro, stemmed

½ pound bean sprouts

1 cup (4½ ounces) chopped unsalted, roasted peanuts

2 cups Sweet-and-Sour Fish Sauce (page 23)

10 skewers

Slice the pork into ½ x 3-inch strips. Use a tenderizer to pound pork. In a bowl, combine the pork with the soy sauce, fish sauce, oyster sauce, hoisin sauce, garlic, onion, green onion, lemongrass, and black pepper. Mix well. Cover and refrigerate for at least 3 hours.

Skewer the meat onto 10 skewers. Cook the meat over a hot grill for approximately 15 minutes, or until the pork is golden brown.

Divide the noodles between four bowls. Top with the meat, a few mint leaves, cilantro, a handful of bean sprouts, and 2 teaspoons of peanuts. Pour 2 to 3 tablespoons of Sweet-and-Sour Fish Sauce over each serving.

Tips: The meat can also be baked in an oven or sautéed in a frying pan.
Baking: Preheat the oven to 350°F. Spread the meat on a baking sheet. Bake for approximately 25 minutes, or until golden brown.
Frying: Heat 1 tablespoon of oil in a nonstick frying pan over medium-high heat. Place the meat in the pan in a single layer. Cook until golden brown, turning the meat occasionally.

Glass Noodle Soup

Canh Miến Thịt Heo

4 servings

Canh miến thịt heo *is a quick and simple noodle dish often served for break-fast in Vietnam. This dish is a slight modification of* canh miến thịt gà *featuring ground pork in place of chicken. Other ground meats, such as turkey, beef, or chicken, may be used instead of pork.*

4 (1.8-ounce) bundles bean thread noodles (miến)

½ cup chopped dried black mushrooms

1 tablespoon vegetable oil

10 ounces lean ground pork

¼ cup finely chopped onion

2 cubes chicken-flavored bouillon

1 teaspoon salt

2 tablespoons fish sauce

½ cup finely chopped green onion

¼ cup finely chopped fresh cilantro

⅛ teaspoon black pepper

Soak the noodles and dried mushrooms in sepa-rate bowls of hot water for 10 minutes. Drain. Cut the noodles into 3-inch lengths.

In a large saucepan, heat the oil over medium-high heat. Add the ground pork and onion, and stir for 2 minutes. Add 2½ quarts of water and bring to a boil, then reduce the heat to medium-low. Simmer for another 10 minutes. Skim the fat from the broth. Stir in the mushrooms, bouillon cubes, salt, and fish sauce. Cook for 10 minutes. Taste and adjust with additional salt if necessary. Remove the saucepan from the heat.

To avoid overcooking the noodles, bring the broth to a boil 10 minutes before serving. Add the noodles and cook for 3 minutes. Remove the saucepan from the heat. (Warning: *Miến* noodles expand and absorb the soup very quickly if over-cooked or are allow to sit for more than 10 min-utes.) Add the green onion, cilantro, and black pepper to the soup.

Serve with Steamed Rice (page 61) or as an appetizer. This soup tastes best when served hot.

Meatball Noodle Soup

Bún Mọc

4 servings

Bún mọc is often eaten for breakfast. The doughless dumplings, known as mọc, are marinated meatballs and served with hot chili sauce (tương ớt) and/or hoisin sauce.

Mix the ground meat with the baking powder, 5 teaspoons of the fish sauce, sugar, potato flakes, oil, black pepper, and 1 tablespoon water in a bowl. Cover and refrigerate for at least 3 hours. Finely regrind the meat in a food processor for 1 minute. Cover and refrigerate until ready to cook.

Place the chicken in a large saucepan with water to cover. Bring to a boil over high heat, then drain. This helps clean the chicken and reduce excess fat.

Return the chicken to the saucepan. Add 8 cups of water and the broth. Bring to a boil over high heat, then reduce the heat to medium and cook for 40 minutes. Transfer the chicken to a bowl, shred into bite-size pieces and set aside.

Add the remaining tablespoon of fish sauce, the bouillon cubes, and onion to the broth. Bring to a boil.

Place teaspoons of the ground meat mixture into the boiling broth. Cook for 10 minutes, or until the dumplings float to the surface. Remove the saucepan from the heat. Add the ginger, green onion, and cilantro to the broth.

1 pound ground chicken, turkey, pork, or beef

1 teaspoon baking powder

1 tablespoon plus 5 teaspoons fish sauce

1 teaspoon sugar

1 tablespoon potato flakes

2 tablespoons vegetable oil

⅛ teaspoon black pepper

2 pounds chicken legs, thighs, and/or wings

2 cubes chicken-flavored bouillon

1 small to medium-size onion, finely chopped

1 teaspoon finely chopped fresh ginger

½ cup finely chopped green onion

½ cup finely chopped fresh cilantro

1 (16-ounce) package rice stick noodles (bún) cooked (page 64)

1 lemon, sliced into wedges

Chili sauce (tương ớt) (optional)

Hoisin sauce (optional)

Divide the *bún* noodles among four bowls. Pour the hot broth and dumplings on top of the noodles. You may add the shredded chicken to the soup or reserve it for a future use, such as Lemon Chicken Salad (page 54). Add the cilantro, green onion, and a few squirts of lemon juice to each bowl. Add hot chili sauce and hoisin sauce according to each person's preference.

Tip: If you do not want to serve chicken in the soup, you may replace it with 2 (14-ounce) cans chicken broth, reducing the water to 8 cups. Some canned chicken broth contains MSG and a high sodium content. Read the label carefully.

Shrimp Noodle Soup

Bún Riêu *4 servings.*

Bún riêu *shrimp noodle soup is another great dish to enjoy for breakfast, lunch, or dinner. The main ingredients are rice field crabs called* cua đồng. *However, in America, rice field crabs are not widely available. The best substitute is ocean crab; the least expensive substitute is dried shrimp and eggs. With these ingredients, quality and flavor are not compromised. Bác Kít's* bún riêu *is a combination of dried shrimp, eggs, rice noodles, and such vegetables as bean sprouts, tomatoes, and mint leaves.*

Rinse and drain the dried shrimp thoroughly. In a large saucepan, combine the shrimp with 2 cups of water. Bring to a boil over high heat, then reduce the heat to low and simmer for 10 minutes. Remove the saucepan from the heat.

Transfer the shrimp to a food processor, leaving the cooking liquid in the saucepan. Grind the shrimp into a fine paste. In a bowl, combine the ground shrimp with the eggs, green onions, and black pepper. Mix well and set aside.

Combine 8 cups of water with the shrimp water in the saucepan. Add the fish sauce, tamarind seasoning, bouillon cubes, and salt. Bring to a boil over high heat. Add half of tomato wedges and ¼ cup of the onion to the broth. Reduce the heat to medium.

Heat the oil in a frying pan over high heat. (Warning: the oil may splatter when hot.) Stir in the remaining ¼ cup of the onion and sauté until golden brown. Add the remaining tomato. Cook, stirring, for 2 minutes. Remove the pan from the heat.

Pour the tomato and onion mixture into the broth. Bring to a boil. Once boiling, stir continuously. Slowly pour in the shrimp and egg mixture, which should float to the surface. Allow the broth to cook for 5 more minutes. Remove the saucepan from the heat.

A Vietnamese Kitchen

1½ cups dried shrimp

2 eggs

¼ cup finely chopped green onion

⅛ teaspoon black pepper

2 tablespoons fish sauce

1 tablespoon tamarind soup base seasoning

2 cubes chicken-flavored bouillon

1 teaspoon salt

2 large tomatoes, sliced into thin wedges

½ cup finely chopped onion

2 tablespoons vegetable oil

1 (16-ounce) package rice stick noodles (bún), cooked (page 64)

½ pound bean sprouts

1 bunch mint, stemmed

½ lemon, quartered

½ bunch Vietnamese water spinach (ung choy), shredded (optional)

2 teaspoons shrimp paste (mắm tôm) (optional)

Fresh Thai peppers (optional)

Divide the *bún* noodles between four serving bowls. Pour the broth over the noodles and add the desired amount of bean sprouts and mint. Add a few squirts of lemon juice to each bowl.

Serve with Vietnamese spinach, hot peppers, and shrimp paste. *Mắm tôm* shrimp paste is one of many popular Vietnamese condiments. It is an acquired taste; serve exclusively to adventurous souls.

Shrimp Chow Mein

Mì Xào Tôm

Mì xào tôm is a soft noodle dish stir-fried with shrimp. Although, this dish is heavily influenced by Chinese cuisine, the Vietnamese have added fish sauce to the equation. Mì xào tôm is yet another example of Vietnam's adapting other cuisines to its own taste.

Mì xào tôm is primarily sold by restaurants and street vendors in Vietnam, but this recipe is simple enough for anyone to prepare. It is a treat.

Shrimp:

2 pounds shrimp, heads and tails removed, peeled and deveined (page 166)

1 tablespoon fish sauce

1 tablespoon oyster sauce

1 tablespoon hoisin sauce

⅛ teaspoon black pepper

For the shrimp: Combine the shrimp with the fish sauce, oyster sauce, hoisin sauce, and black pepper in a bowl. Cover and refrigerate for at least 15 minutes, or until ready to cook.

Chow Mein:

2 medium carrots, peeled and sliced diagonally

½ pound broccoli, cut into bite-size pieces

½ pound snow peas or sugar peas, trimmed

1 (14-ounce) package egg noodles (mì), steamed

3 tablespoons soy sauce

1 tablespoon oyster sauce

1 tablespoon hoisin sauce

2 tablespoons vegetable oil

1 teaspoon finely chopped garlic

1 medium-size onion, cut into 16 wedges

4 ounces fresh mushrooms, halved

½ cup finely chopped green onion

½ cup finely chopped fresh cilantro

⅛ teaspoon black pepper

½ teaspoon chili or pepper sauce (optional)

For the chow mein: Bring 5 cups of water to a boil in a saucepan over high heat. Add the carrots and cook for 1 minute. Add the broccoli and peas and cook for 1 more minute. Remove the saucepan from the heat. Transfer the vegetables to a colander, rinse them under cold water, and drain.

In the same saucepan, bring 8 cups of water to a boil over high heat. Add the noodles and cook for 3 minutes to reheat them. Transfer the noodles to a colander or sieve. Rinse them under cold water to prevent them from sticking together. Drain.

In a small bowl, combine the soy sauce, oyster sauce, and hoisin sauce. Mix well and set aside. Heat 1 tablespoon of the oil in a frying pan over high heat for 1 to 2 minutes. Add the garlic and onion, and stir until golden brown. Add the shrimp and cook, stirring, for 2 minutes. Add the cooked vegetables, mushrooms, and soy sauce mixture, and cook, stirring, for 2 more minutes. Transfer the shrimp mixture to a bowl.

In the same frying pan, heat the remaining 1 tablespoon of oil over high heat. Add the noodles and stir continuously for 2 minutes, then stir in the shrimp mixture, and slowly pour in 1 cup of water. Cook, stirring, for 1 more minute. Remove the frying pan from the heat. Add the green onion, cilantro, black pepper and the chili sauce.

Tip: You may substitute 2 pounds other seafood or 1 pound of beef, chicken, or pork for the shrimp. Use the marinated meat recipe (page 132) to marinate beef, chicken, or pork. Increase the cooking time for pork and chicken to 3 minutes and decrease the cooking time for beef to 1 minute.

Stir-fries

Stir-fried dishes, known as *xào* in Vietnamese, are frequently served with soup, *kho* dishes, and steamed rice. Stir-fries are fried quickly in a wok or a nonstick frying pan with a little or no oil. The following recipes offer basic instructions on how to prepare various vegetables and meats by this method. Once you are familiar with the fundamentals, you may substitute different vegetables and meats. Do not forget to adjust the amount of seasonings to your liking. If you already have experience with this style of Asian cooking, these recipes provide the basics to make your stir-fries taste uniquely Vietnamese.

A stir-fry with large quantity of meat such as Tomato Sautéed Beef (page 105) is usually reserved for a weekly treat or for celebrations. Meat is expensive in Vietnam so it is always an occasion when it is served. Other vegetable stir-fries such as Sautéed Tofu (page 103) or Crispy Stir-Fried Bean Sprouts (page 91) are commonly served everyday.

Stir-fries are quick and easy to make. Generally, a simple stir-fry will take at most 20 to 30 minutes to make. You can stir-fry practically any vegetables or meat. One draw back of stir-fries is that they get cold very quickly. Hence, my motto is "eat it while it is hot."

Crispy Stir-Fried Bean Sprouts

Gía Xào

2 servings

Giá xào is yet another simple stir-fry. Bean sprouts do not have a strong taste, but absorb the flavor of the sauce. Beef is a good complement for bean sprouts, but chicken, turkey, pork, or shrimp, can also be used. You may also replace the bean sprouts with other leafy green vegetables, such as bok choy, cabbage, or spinach. Since they are crispy and light, bean sprouts digest well, leave room for dessert.

½ pound beef sirloin, thinly sliced or ground

½ onion, cut into 6 wedges

1 tablespoon oyster sauce

2 tablespoons soy sauce

3 tablespoons vegetable oil

1 teaspoon finely chopped garlic

1 pound bean sprouts

¼ cup green onion, finely chopped

¼ cup fresh cilantro, finely chopped

⅛ teaspoon black pepper

In a bowl, combine the beef with the onion, oyster sauce, and soy sauce. Cover and refrigerate for at least 15 minutes.

Heat 1 tablespoon of the oil in a large frying pan or wok over medium-high heat. Add the garlic and stir until lightly golden brown. Add the beef and stir for 1 minute (the meat should be rare). Transfer the meat mixture to a bowl.

Heat the remaining 2 tablespoons of oil in the same pan. Stir in the bean sprouts and cook for 1 minute over medium-high heat. Mix in the meat mixture and stir for 1 minute. Remove the frying pan from the heat. Mix in the chopped green onion and cilantro. Sprinkle black pepper on top. Serve with Steamed Rice (page 61).

Crispy Stir-Fried Noodles

Mì Xào Dòn

4 to 6 servings

Mì xào dòn, *made with crispy egg noodles, beef, vegetables, and a special marinated sauce, is not as common as many other noodle dishes but it is one of my favorites. It is not frequently prepared at home; my first encounter with this dish was in a Vietnamese restaurant in America. The sauce is the most important component because it complements the crispy noodles and vegetables. Other meats and/or seafood may be used instead of the beef.*

Preheat the oven to 350°F. Spread the steamed egg noodles on an ungreased baking sheet. Bake for 10 minutes. Turn the noodles and bake for 3 more minutes. Turn off the oven. Leave the noodles in the oven until ready to serve.

Bring 4 cups of water to a boil in a saucepan over high heat. Add the carrots to the boiling water and cook for 1 minute. Add the broccoli and peas, and cook for 1 minute. Transfer the vegetables to a strainer, leaving the liquid in the saucepan. Add the bok choy to the liquid and cook for 1 more minute over high heat. Remove the bok choy from the liquid. Rinse the vegetables under cold water and drain.

Leave the remaining liquid simmering in the saucepan over medium-high heat. Add the bouillon, 1 tablespoon of the soy sauce, 1 tablespoon of oyster sauce, and ⅛ teaspoon of the black pepper. Combine the cornstarch, flour, and ½ cup of water in a small bowl. Mix well. Slowly stir the flour mixture into the broth. Cook, stirring, for 1 minute, or until the gravy thickens. Reduce the heat to a low simmer.

Combine the remaining tablespoon of soy sauce, remaining tablespoon of oyster sauce, the hoisin sauce, and the fish sauce in a small bowl. Mix well.

1 (14-ounce) package egg noodles (mì), steamed

2 medium carrots, peeled and sliced diagonally

½ pound broccoli, cut into bite-size pieces

½ pound snow peas or sugar snap peas, trimmed

1 pound (4 to 5) baby bok choy, sliced lengthwise into 2 or 3 pieces

1 cube chicken-flavored bouillon

2 tablespoons soy sauce

2 tablespoons oyster sauce

¼ teaspoon black pepper

2 tablespoons cornstarch

1 tablespoon all-purpose flour

1 tablespoon hoisin sauce

1 tablespoon fish sauce

5 teaspoons vegetable oil

1 pound marinated beef (page 132)

1 medium-size onion, cut into thin wedges

4 ounces fresh mushrooms, halved

½ cup finely chopped green onion

½ cup finely chopped fresh cilantro

½ teaspoon chili or pepper sauce (optional)

Heat 2 teaspoons of the oil in a frying pan over high heat for 1 to 2 minutes. Add the marinated beef and stir for 1 minute then transfer to a plate. Add the remaining 3 teaspoons of oil to the same pan. Add the onion and stir for 30 seconds. Add the mushrooms and then the cooked vegetables and soy sauce mixture. Cook, stirring, for 2 minutes.

Meanwhile, increase the heat under the sauce to medium-high and bring it to a boil. Add the beef to the vegetables. Cook, stirring, for 1 more minute.

Once the sauce is boiling, pour it over the beef and vegetables. Mix well. Remove the frying pan from the heat. Add the green onion, cilantro and ⅛ teaspoon of the black pepper.

Divide the noodles between four to six plates. Place 3 pieces of bok choy around the edge of the noodles. Place the beef and vegetables on top. For spicy food lovers, add the chili sauce to heighten the zestiness of this dish.

Sizzling Stir-fried Bok Choy

Xào Cải Ngọt Và Thịt

Xào cải ngọt và thịt *is an effortless dish. This dish is a combination of bok choy and sliced tender beef in a flavorful marinade. You may use either or both regular or baby bok choy.*

2 tablespoons vegetable oil
2 tablespoons finely chopped onion
½ pound marinated top sirloin beef (page 132)
1 pound bok choy or baby bok choy, cut into 1-inch pieces
1 tablespoon oyster sauce
2 tablespoons soy sauce

Heat 1 tablespoon of the oil in a frying pan or wok over high heat for 1 to 2 minutes. Add the onion and stir until lightly golden brown. Add the marinated beef and stir for 1 minute. Transfer the meat mixture to a bowl.

Heat the remaining tablespoon of oil in the same pan for 1 minute over medium-high. Add the bok choy and cook, stirring occasionally, for 3 minutes. Add the oyster sauce, soy sauce, and meat, and stir for 1 more minute. Remove the frying pan from the heat. Serve with Steamed Rice (page 61).

Stir-fried Cauliflower and Broccoli

Bông Cải Xào

Cauliflower was one of my favorite vegetables when I was growing up in Vietnam. I do not recall having broccoli until I came to America, however, it quickly became one of my favorites. This dish was created to combine my two favorite vegetables. It symbolizes a blend of my two favorite cultures.

1 tablespoon vegetable oil

1 teaspoon minced garlic

6 ounces marinated beef, chicken, or pork, ground or thinly sliced (page 132)

½ head cauliflower, cut into bite-size pieces

½ head broccoli, cut into bite-size pieces

8 ounces fresh mushrooms, thinly sliced

½ teaspoon salt

1 tablespoon fish sauce

⅛ teaspoon black pepper

Heat the oil in a frying pan over medium-high heat. Add the garlic. Cook, stirring, until lightly golden. Add the meat. Stir-fry for 1 minute or until no longer pink. Mix in the cauliflower, broccoli, and mushrooms. Stir-fry for 2 minutes. Add salt, fish sauce, and ¼ cup of water. Reduce the heat to medium, cover and cook for 5 to 10 minutes or until the broccoli and cauliflower soften. Adjust with additional salt if necessary.

Remove from the heat. Sprinkle the pepper over the vegetables. Serve with Steamed Rice (page 61).

Stir-Fried Eggplant

Cà Tím Xào

This is a simple recipe yet not traditionally Vietnamese because the meat is not marinated and there is no fish sauce. The eggplant melts in your mouth and leaves a scent of garlic behind. Stir-fried eggplant tastes even better on the second day.

1 tablespoon vegetable oil

1 teaspoon minced garlic

½ cup chopped onion

6 ounces boneless chicken breasts, thinly sliced or ground

1 teaspoon salt

1 pound long purple eggplants, sliced diagonally ¼ inch thick

1 tomato, cut into 16 wedges

⅛ teaspoon black pepper

¼ cup chopped tía tô mint (optional)

Heat the oil in a frying pan over medium-high heat. Add the garlic and the onion. Cook, stirring, until lightly golden. Add the chicken and ¼ teaspoon salt. Stir-fry for 3 to 5 minutes or until the chicken is no longer pink, then add the eggplant and tomato. Cook, stirring for 1 minute. Pour in ½ cup of water and bring to a boil. Reduce the heat to medium. Mix in the remaining salt. Cover and cook for 5 minutes or until the eggplant softens.

Remove from the heat. Sprinkle the pepper and the *tía tô* mint over the eggplant. Serve with Steamed Rice (page 61).

Stir-Fried Green Beans

Thịt Xào Đậu Que

Thịt xào đậu que is green beans stir-fried with seasoned meat. Beef, pork, chicken, or turkey may be used for this recipe. This dish is fast and tasty.

---

2 tablespoons soy sauce

⅛ teaspoon salt

½ pound marinated beef, pork, chicken, or turkey, thinly sliced or ground (page 132)

1 pound green beans, trimmed and halved lengthwise

4 teaspoons vegetable oil

⅛ teaspoon black pepper

In a small bowl, combine the soy sauce, salt, and ½ cup of water.

Heat 2 teaspoons of the oil in a large nonstick frying pan or wok over high heat. Heat the oil until it begins to smoke. (Warning: Turn on the stove vent to "high" to prevent those pesky smoke alarms from going off.)

Add the green beans to the oil and stir for 3 minutes. Add the soy sauce mixture and stir for 3 more minutes. Transfer the green beans to a bowl.

Heat the remaining 2 teaspoons of oil in the same pan for 1 to 2 minutes over medium-high heat. Add the marinated meat and stir for 1 to 2 minutes, or until no longer pink. Add the green beans and stir for 1 more minute. Remove the frying pan or wok from the heat. Sprinkle black pepper on top. Serve with Steamed Rice (page 61).

Stir-fries

Stir-Fried Pickled Greens

Dưa Chua Xào

4 servings

Dưa chua sào *is a stir-fried dish that combines Pickled Mustard Greens (page 26), meat, and tomatoes. The northern Vietnamese country folk love this dish. They often prepare* dưa chua xào *with the cheapest cuts of meat, such as intestines or other variety meats. Yes, you have read correctly. Intestines, hearts, gizzards, and other offal are considered a delicacy in Vietnam. Once again, nothing goes to waste.*

¼ recipe Pickled Chinese Mustard Greens (dưa chua) *(page 26)*

3 tablespoons vegetable oil

2 tablespoons finely chopped onion

2 medium-size tomatoes, sliced into wedges

2 tablespoons fish sauce

1 pound marinated chicken, turkey, pork, or beef, ground or thinly sliced *(page 132)*

¼ cup finely chopped green onion

¼ cup finely chopped rau ôm *mint, stemmed (optional)*

Rinse the *dưa chua* in cold water, then squeeze and drain thoroughly. Heat 2 tablespoons of the oil in a saucepan over high heat for 1 to 2 minutes. Add the onion and stir until golden brown. Stir in the *dưa chua* and tomatoes, and cook for 10 minutes. Add ½ cup of water. Bring to a boil, then reduce the heat to low and stir in the fish sauce. Cook for 5 minutes.

Meanwhile, heat the remaining 1 tablespoon of oil in a large frying pan over high heat. Add the marinated meat. Cook, stirring, for 3 to 5 minutes, or until the meat is no longer pink. Remove the frying pan from the heat.

Add the meat to the *dưa chua*. Cook, stirring, for 1 minute Then remove the saucepan from the heat. Add the green onion and *rau ôm* mint. Serve with Steamed Rice (page 61).

Tips: The cooking time for pork or chicken is 5 minutes, while that for beef is 3 minutes.

Stir-fried Potatoes

Khoai Tây Xào

2 to 4 servings

Stir-fried potatoes are the Vietnamese version of French fries. There was no such thing as French fries when I was growing up in Vietnam, but these were a great substitute. Whenever my mom made stir-fried potatoes, I always stole a few. Thinner slices make for a crunchier bite. Yum!

6 red potatoes, peeled and thinly sliced

3 cups vegetable oil

1 teaspoon minced garlic

1 onion, cut into 12 wedges

6 ounces marinated beef, chicken, or pork, ground or thinly sliced (page 132)

4 ounces fresh mushrooms, thinly sliced

¼ teaspoon salt

4 teaspoons fish sauce

¼ cup finely chopped fresh cilantro

⅛ teaspoon black pepper

Heat the oil in a deep frying pan over medium-high heat. Fry the potatoes until lightly golden. Transfer to a plate lined with paper towels. Reserve 1 tablespoon of oil in the pan.

Heat the reserved oil in the pan over medium-high heat. Add the garlic and onion. Cook, stirring, until lightly golden. Add the meat. Stir-fry for 3 minutes or until no longer pink. Mix in the mushrooms and stir-fry for 1 minute. Add the potatoes, salt, fish sauce, and ¼ cup of water. Cook, stirring for 1 more minute. Adjust with additional salt if necessary.

Remove from the heat. Sprinkle the cilantro and black pepper over the stir-fry. Serve with Steamed Rice (page 61).

Stir-fries

Stir-Fried Vietnamese Spinach

Rau Muống Xào

You may substitute American spinach for the ung choy in this dish, but be aware that American spinach differs in texture and appearance. Vietnamese spinach has larger and longer stems and is less leafy than American spinach. The stems are crunchy and leaves are soft and chewy.

This dish is a popular poor man's food in Vietnam because it is inexpensive to grow in the humid climate. Ironically, in the States Vietnamese spinach is pricey because of high demand and low supply. Over the past few years though, Vietnamese spinach is slowly increasing in supply. Eventually, the price will decline. This spinach may be found in Asian supermarkets.

½ bunch (15 ounces) Vietnamese water spinach (ung choy)

2 teaspoons fish sauce

2 teaspoons soy sauce

2 teaspoons oyster sauce

2 tablespoons oil

2 tablespoons finely chopped onion

6 ounces marinated beef sirloin, thinly sliced (page 132) (optional)

1 teaspoon finely chopped garlic

⅛ teaspoon black pepper

¼ cup finely chopped Thai basil (húng phở)

2 teaspoons lemon juice

½ bunch rau ôm mint, finely chopped (optional)

Rinse and drain the spinach thoroughly. Remove any wilted leaves. Cut the spinach into 2- to 3-inch lengths. Combine the fish sauce, soy sauce, and oyster sauce in a small bowl. Mix well.

Heat 1 tablespoon of the oil in a large nonstick frying pan or wok for 1 to 2 minutes over medium-high heat. Add the onion and stir until golden brown. Add the beef and stir for 1 minute. Mix in the spinach and stir for 2 minutes. Add the fish sauce mixture and stir for 1 minute. Remove the frying pan from the heat. Mix in the remaining 1 tablespoon of oil, garlic, black pepper, basil, lemon juice, and *rau ôm* mint. Serve with Steamed Rice (page 61).

Stuffed Tofu

Đậu Hủ Nhồi

Stuffed tofu is a meaty tofu dish. The meat enhances the tofu's flavor and the sautéed onion and tomato provide a subtle hint of sweetness and sourness.

¼ cup chopped dried black mushrooms

½ ounce bean thread noodles, (miến)

8 ounces ground turkey, chicken, beef, or pork

½ teaspoon salt

¼ teaspoon black pepper

1 (12- to 14-ounce) package firm tofu

1 cup vegetable oil

½ onion, cut into 6 wedges

2 medium-size tomatoes, each cut into 12 wedges

1 tablespoon fish sauce

Soak the dried mushrooms and noodles in separate bowls of hot water for 10 minutes. Drain. Cut the noodles into 1-inch lengths.

In a medium-size bowl, combine the ground meat with the mushrooms, noodles, salt, and black pepper. Cover and refrigerate for at least 15 minutes.

Soak the tofu in hot water for 15 to 30 minutes or heat in a microwave on HIGH for 30 to 60 seconds. (Warm tofu is firmer and easier to fry. Draining the tofu reduces the splattering when frying.) Slice into 1 x 2-inch pieces that are ¾ inch thick. It is important that the tofu is thick enough so you can stuff it.

Heat the oil in a frying pan or wok over medium-high heat. (Warning: The oil may splatter when hot.) Place the tofu in the pan in a single layer. You may need to cook the tofu in batches. Fry the tofu until lightly golden. Transfer to a plate and use paper towels to absorb excess oil. Reserve 1 tablespoon of oil in the pan.

Form ½-inch balls with the meat. Cut a small slit on the side of the tofu. Stuff the meat ball into the opening.

Heat the oil in a frying pan over medium-high heat. Add the onion and stir until lightly golden. Add the tomato and stir for 2 minutes. Add the tofu, meat, fish sauce, and any extra meatballs or tofu. Reduce the heat to medium, cover and cook for 15 minutes or until the meat is no longer pink.

Remove from the heat. Serve with Steamed Rice (page 61).

Tofu Curry

Đậu Hủ Xào Sả Ca-ri

2 to 4 servings

Curried tofu is a great vegan dish. Although tofu is a great source of protein, it was not a common dish served in my family. I did not like tofu or curry when I was growing up but now I crave them.

I am not a fan of spicy food so this recipe has been modified to make it less spicy than most versions by using mild curry powder. Feel free to replace it with a spicier version.

---

1 (12 to 14-ounce) package firm tofu

1 cup vegetable oil

1 tablespoon finely chopped lemongrass

1 tablespoon mild curry powder

¼ cup soy sauce

1 tablespoon sugar

⅛ teaspoon black pepper

Soak the tofu in hot water for 15 to 30 minutes or heat in a microwave on HIGH for 30 to 60 seconds. (Warm tofu is firmer and easier to fry. Draining the tofu reduces the splattering when frying.) Slice into rectangular bite-size pieces.

Heat the oil in a frying pan or wok over medium-high heat. (Warning: The oil may splatter when hot.) Place the tofu in the pan in a single layer. You may need to cook the tofu in batches. Fry until lightly golden. Transfer to a plate and use paper towels to absorb excess oil. Reserve 1 tablespoon of oil in the pan.

Combine the tofu, lemongrass, curry, soy sauce, sugar, and black pepper in a bowl. Mix well. Cover and refrigerate for at least 3 hours or overnight.

Heat the reserved oil in the pan over medium-high heat. Add the tofu and its

marinade. Stir-fry for 5 minutes. Add ¼ cup of water if the pan is dry. Stir-fry for 1 more minute or until the water has soaked into the tofu.

Remove from the heat. Serve with Steamed Rice (page 61).

Sautéed Tofu

Đậu Hủ Sốt Cà Chua

Đậu hủ sốt cà chua is a very simple tofu dish sautéed with juicy tomatoes, onion, and spices. It can be easily converted to a vegetarian dish by simply replacing the fish sauce with soy sauce.

---

1 (12 to 14-ounce) package firm tofu

1 cup vegetable oil

2 teaspoons soy sauce

2 teaspoons fish sauce

1 teaspoon mushroom seasoning (optional)

½ onion, cut into wedges

2 tomatoes, cut into wedges

¼ cup finely chopped green onion

½ cup finely chopped fresh cilantro

⅛ teaspoon black pepper

Soak the tofu in hot water for 15 to 30 minutes, or heat in a microwave oven on HIGH for 30 to 60 seconds. Drain thoroughly on several paper towels before frying. (Warm tofu is firmer and easier to fry. Draining the tofu reduces the splattering when frying.) Cut the tofu into rectangular bite-size pieces.

Heat the oil in a large nonstick frying pan or wok over medium-high heat. (Warning: The oil may splatter when hot.) Place the tofu in the pan in a single layer. The frying may need to be done in batches. Fry the tofu until lightly golden. Transfer to a plate lined with paper towels to absorb excess oil. Reserve 1 teaspoon of oil in the pan.

In a small bowl, combine the soy sauce, fish sauce, mushroom seasoning, and ½ cup of water. Heat the reserved oil in the pan for 1 to 2 minutes. Add the onion, and stir over medium-high heat until golden brown. Add the tomatoes and stir for 2 minutes. Add the tofu and soy sauce mixture, and stir for 2 more minutes. Remove the pan from the heat. Top the tofu with the green onion, cilantro, and black pepper. Serve with Steamed Rice (page 61).

Tips: ½ pound of marinated ground or thinly sliced pork, beef or chicken (page 132) can be added with the onions. Stir for 2 to 3 minutes, or until the meat is no longer pink. Add the tomatoes and proceed with the recipe.

Prefrying the tofu is not necessary, but it prevents the tofu from falling apart during cooking. Fried tofu also tastes better.

Stir-fries

Egg Sautéed Tofu

Đậu Hủ Sốt Cà Chua với trứng

4 servings

Đậu hủ sốt cà chua với trứng *is tofu sautéed with eggs, tomatoes, and onion. This dish provides a good source of protein without any red meat. For an even healthier dish, use egg whites instead of whole eggs.*

1 (12 to 14-ounce) package firm tofu

½ cup finely chopped green onion

2 eggs, lightly beaten

1 cup vegetable oil

2 teaspoons soy sauce

2 teaspoons fish sauce

½ onion, cut into wedges

2 tomatoes, cut into wedges

½ cup finely chopped fresh cilantro

⅛ teaspoon black pepper

Soak the tofu in hot water for 15 to 30 minutes or heat in a microwave oven on HIGH for 30 to 60 seconds. Drain and dry the tofu thoroughly on paper towels before frying. (Warm tofu is firmer and easier to fry. Draining the tofu reduces the splattering when frying.) Cut the tofu into rectangular bite-size pieces. Mix ¼ cup of the green onions with the eggs.

Heat the oil in a large nonstick frying pan or wok over medium-high heat. (Warning: The oil may splatter when hot.) Place the tofu in the pan in a single layer. You may need to cook the tofu in batches. Fry the tofu until lightly golden. Transfer to a plate and use paper towels to absorb excess oil. Reserve 1 teaspoon of oil in the pan.

Combine the soy sauce, fish sauce, and ½ cup of water in a small bowl. Heat the reserved oil over medium-high heat for 1 to 2 minutes. Add the onion and sauté until golden brown. Add the tomatoes and stir for 2 minutes. Mix in the tofu and the soy sauce mixture, and stir for 2 more minutes. Add the egg mixture and stir for 1 minute. Remove the frying pan from the heat. Top with the remaining green onion, the cilantro, and black pepper. Serve with Steamed Rice (page 61).

Tip: Prefrying the tofu is not necessary, but it prevents the tofu from falling apart during cooking. Fried tofu also tastes better.

A Vietnamese Kitchen

Tomato Sautéed Beef

Thịt Bò Sốt Cà Chua

Thịt bò sốt cà chua *was Bác Kít's mother's special recipe. This dish was quite a treat on Sundays when she was growing up in northern Vietnam. The aroma of sautéed garlic and tomatoes would envelop the kitchen. She has adapted her mother's recipe, adding her own special touches with ingredients available in America.*

1 pound marinated beef sirloin (page 132)

2 tablespoons vegetable oil

1 teaspoon garlic

1 medium-size onion, sliced into small wedges

1 tablespoon fish sauce

1 tablespoon soy sauce

1 teaspoon sugar

2 large tomatoes, cut into 8 wedges edges

½ cup finely chopped green onions

½ cup finely chopped fresh cilantro

⅛ teaspoon black pepper

1 teaspoon lemon juice

Heat 1 tablespoon of the oil in a large nonstick frying pan for 1 to 2 minutes over high heat. Add the garlic and onion. Stir for 1 minute, or until lightly golden brown. Add the marinated beef and stir for 2 minutes. Transfer the meat mixture to a bowl.

Combine the fish sauce, soy sauce, sugar, and ½ cup of water in a separate bowl. Mix well. Heat the remaining tablespoon of oil in the same pan for 1 minute over high heat. Add the tomatoes and stir for 1 minute. Add the fish sauce mixture and stir for 1 minute. Mix in the meat mixture and stir for 2 minutes. Remove the frying pan from the heat.

Mix the green onion, cilantro, black pepper, and lemon juice into the sautéed beef. Serve with Steamed Rice (page 61), salad, or bread.

Kho *Dishes*

Kho is a term for dishes braised or stewed in brine. Northern Vietnamese country folks frequently serve *kho* dishes made with fish sauce, water, salt, sugar and garlic. Although these dishes are very salty, the marinade enhances the natural sweetness and saltiness of meats, seafood, tofu, and vegetables.

Kho was a common meal for Bác Kít when she was growing up on a farm. Braising and stewing methods helped many farmers to survive through such hardships as flood and famine. The meat's flavor is so strong that you only need or want a little bit at a time. Therefore the meat can be eaten over several days. Keep in mind that refrigeration was not affordable or available to the country folks. The *kho* method also helped preserve the meat.

The following recipes are not be as salty as those traditionally served, because it is not healthy to consume so much salt. Although, *kho* is no longer as salty as traditionally intended, preparing it is still a lengthy process. Vietnamese cooks often intentionally make large quantities for leftovers to be eaten over several days. It tastes even better reheated.

Traditionally, *kho* is stewed in a clay pot over hot coals. If you don't have a clay pot, a saucepan is a great substitute. To prepare a basic *kho* dish, simply combine all the ingredients in a saucepan and allow it to simmer until two thirds of the juice has evaporated. Another critical ingredient of a *kho* dish is browning sauce or *Kẹo đắng* (page 24). *Kẹo đắng* is caramelized sugar cooked to a dark and bittersweet sauce, which balances the saltiness of the fish sauce. The dark brown color of *kẹo đắng* adds a pleasant reddish brown hue to whatever is being cooked.

You can also find *kho* stew in Chinese restaurants, as it is popular in southern China. The recipes in this chapter are fundamental *kho* meat, seafood, tofu and vegetable dishes. Once you are comfortable with these recipes, have fun experimenting with different ingredients, such as lamb.

Sautéed Zucchini Stew

Bí Kho   *2 servings*

Bí kho is a simple vegetarian kho *dish of zucchini simmered in soy sauce. Other summer squash may be used instead. Bác Kít occasionally donated her time to help cook in a Buddhist temple.* Bí kho *was usually one of the Buddhist monks' requests.*

⅓ cup vegetable oil

2 medium-size zucchini, peeled and sliced into ½-inch disks

2 tablespoons soy sauce

1 teaspoon sugar

⅛ teaspoon pepper

Heat the oil in a large frying pan for 1 to 2 minutes over medium heat. Make sure the zucchini is completely dry to reduce splattering. Place the squash in a single layer in the frying pan. If necessary, fry them in several batches. Fry the squash for 2 to 3 minutes on each side, or until golden brown. Transfer to a dish lined with paper towels to absorb excess oil.

In a bowl, combine the soy sauce, sugar, black pepper, and ¼ cup of water. Return the squash to the frying pan over medium heat. Pour the soy sauce mixture over it. Cook for 30 seconds, turning the squash so they absorb the sauce evenly. When the liquid boils, reduce the heat to low. Simmer for 5 more minutes, or until two-thirds of the liquid evaporates.

Remove the saucepan from the heat. Serve with Steamed Rice (page 61).

Kho *Dishes*   109

Tofu Stew

Đậu Hủ kho

2 to 4 servings

Tofu makes great kho *because of its ability to absorb flavors quickly. It is also soft so you do not have to stew it for a long period of time. You may also stew the tofu without frying it. However, I find it much easier to handle and tastier when it is fried. For a completely vegan dish, you may replace the fish sauce with additional soy sauce.*

1 (12- to 14-ounce) package tofu

1 cup vegetable oil

⅓ cup chopped onion

1 tablespoon fish sauce

1 tablespoon soy sauce

1 teaspoon mushroom seasoning (optional)

⅛ teaspoon black pepper

Soak the tofu in hot water for 15 to 30 minutes or heat it in a microwave on HIGH for 30 to 60 seconds until warm. Drain thoroughly on several paper towels before frying. (This firms the tofu making it easier to fry. Draining the tofu reduces the splattering when frying.) Cut the tofu into rectangular bite-size pieces.

Heat the oil in a large frying pan or wok over medium-high heat. (Warning: The oil may splatter when hot.) Fry the tofu in a single layer. This may need to be done in batches. Fry the tofu until lightly golden. Transfer to a plate lined with paper towels to absorb excess oil.

Add the onion to the same pan, over high heat. Stir constantly for 2 minutes, or until golden. Add the tofu, fish sauce, soy sauce, mushroom seasoning, and black pepper. Mix well, and stir-fry for 3 minutes. Add 1 cup of water and cook, stirring, for 5 more minutes, or until two-thirds of the water has evaporated.

Remove from the heat. Serve with Steamed Rice (page 61).

110

Clay Pot Tofu with Pork

Đậu Hủ Kho Thịt

2 to 4 servings

Đậu hủ kho thịt consists of marinated pork loin with seasoned fried tofu. Pork contributes a wonderful meaty flavor to tofu. This is a popular dish served in northern Vietnam. It contains plenty of protein and yet it is simple and tasty.

---

1 pound pork loin, thinly sliced

2 tablespoons fish sauce

1 tablespoon oyster sauce

⅓ cup chopped onion

½ teaspoon salt

¼ teaspoon black pepper

1 tablespoon homemade Browning Sauce (page 24), or 1 teaspoon bottled browning and seasoning sauce (such as Kitchen Bouquet)

½ (12-ounce) package tofu

1 cup vegetable oil

Combine the pork with the fish sauce, oyster sauce, onion, salt, pepper, and browning sauce in a bowl. Cover and refrigerate for at least 15 minutes.

Soak the tofu in hot water for 15 to 30 minutes or heat it in a microwave on HIGH for 30 to 60 seconds until warm. Drain thoroughly on several paper towels before frying. (This firms the tofu making it easier to fry. Draining the tofu reduces the splattering when frying.) Cut the tofu into rectangular bite-size pieces.

Heat the oil in a large frying pan or wok over medium-high heat. (Warning: The oil may splatter.) Place the tofu in the pan in a single layer. The frying may need to be done in batches. Fry the tofu until lightly golden. Transfer the tofu to a plate lined with paper towels to absorb excess oil.

In the same frying pan, cook the marinated meat over high heat. Stir constantly for 5 minutes, or until the meat is no longer pink. Add the tofu and 1 cup of water and cook for 7 more minutes.

Remove from the heat. Serve with Steamed Rice (page 61).

Clay Pot Ginger Chicken

Gà Kho Gừng

2 to 4 servings

Gà kho gừng *is another great chicken recipe. The Vietnamese love to gnaw on bones, which contain tasty marrow and cooking juices. In Vietnamese cooking, poultry bones are usually chopped into small chunks, right along with the flesh, to enable diners to suck the bones to their heart's content.*

2 pounds chicken, any parts, with or without skin

1 tablespoon sugar

2 tablespoons fish sauce

1 tablespoon oyster sauce

1 tablespoon soy sauce

2 tablespoons finely chopped fresh ginger

1 teaspoon minced garlic

½ cup chopped onion

½ teaspoon salt

1 tablespoon homemade Browning Sauce (page 24), or 1 teaspoon bottled browning and seasoning sauce (such as Kitchen Bouquet)

¼ teaspoon black pepper

Cut the chicken, including the bones, into 1- to 2-inch chunks. Combine the chicken with the sugar, fish sauce, oyster sauce, ginger, garlic, onion, salt, browning sauce, and pepper in a mixing bowl. Mix well. Cover and refrigerate. Allow to marinate for at least 30 minutes.

Heat a saucepan over high heat. Add the chicken and cook, stirring, for 10 minutes. After 10 minutes, if the pan appears to be dry, pour in 1 cup of water and bring to boil. Reduce the heat to medium and stir occasionally. Cook for 10 more minutes, or until two-thirds of the liquid evaporates.

Remove from the heat. Serve with Steamed Rice (page 61).

Clay Pot Beef Stew

Bò Kho

Bò kho is made from beef sirloin marinated with ginger, garlic, and spices. The marinade adds a sweet-and-sour flavor to the beef, and the stewing process tenderizes the meat. By the time the cooking is complete, the beef will melt in your mouth.

1½ to 2 pounds beef sirloin, round beef, or beef stew

1 tablespoon beef stew spice (gia vi bò kho)*

2 tablespoons sugar

2 tablespoons fish sauce

1 tablespoon oyster sauce

1 tablespoon finely chopped fresh ginger

1 teaspoon minced and chopped garlic

⅓ cup chopped onion

¼ teaspoon salt

¼ teaspoon black pepper

Cut the beef into 1-inch cubes and combine it with the beef stew spice, sugar, fish sauce, oyster sauce, ginger, garlic, onion, salt, and pepper in a large bowl. Cover and refrigerate for at least 30 minutes.

Heat the saucepan over high heat. Add the beef, and cook, stirring, for 7 minutes. Pour in 1 cup of water and reduce the heat to medium. Cook, occasionally stirring, for 1 hour, or until two-thirds of the water evaporates.

Remove from the heat. Serve with Steamed Rice (page 61).

*If *gia vi bò kho* is not available, use 1 teaspoon chili powder, ½ teaspoon paprika, ½ teaspoon minced garlic, ¼ teaspoon onion powder, ¼ teaspoon ground star anise, ¼ teaspoon ground cinnamon, and ¼ teaspoon ground cloves.

Kho *Dishes*

Pork Stew

Thịt Heo Kho

4 servings

Traditionally, Dưa Chua (page 26) and thịt heo kho *go hand in hand making for a salty and sour flavor with a hint of bittersweetness. A northern meal occasionally includes this dish, Dưa Chua, a simple soup, and steamed rice.*

2 pounds pork sirloin or any lean pork

1 tablespoon sugar

2 tablespoons finely chopped onion

3 tablespoons fish sauce

2 tablespoons soy sauce

2 tablespoons oyster sauce

⅛ teaspoon black pepper

1 tablespoon homemade Browning Sauce (page 24), or 1 teaspoon bottled browning and seasoning sauce (such as Kitchen Bouquet)

¼ cup finely chopped green onion

Cut the pork into 1-inch cubes or thin slices, and combine it with the sugar, onion, fish sauce, soy sauce, oyster sauce, black pepper, and browning sauce in a medium-size bowl. Mix well. Cover and refrigerate for at least 30 minutes.

Place the marinated meat in a saucepan. Cook, stirring occasionally, for 10 minutes over medium-high heat. Add ½ cup of water and bring to a boil over high heat. Reduce the heat to medium-low and cook for 10 more minutes, or until two-thirds of the water has evaporated.

Remove the saucepan from the heat. Mix in the green onion. Serve with Steamed Rice (page 61).

A Vietnamese Kitchen

Egg and Pork Stew

Thịt Heo Kho Trứng

Thịt heo kho trứng *is similar to Pork Stew (page 114), but includes eggs. My children love the eggs because they are soaked full of meaty flavor. The pork stew originates from the northern region while the eggs are a special touch added by the south.*

1 pound pork sirloin or any lean pork, cut into 1-inch cubes

4 teaspoons fish sauce

1 tablespoon soy sauce

1 tablespoon oyster sauce

¼ teaspoon salt

1 teaspoon sugar

2 tablespoons finely chopped onion

⅛ teaspoon black pepper

2 tablespoons homemade Browning Sauce (page 24), or 1 teaspoon bottled browning and seasoning sauce (such as Kitchen Bouquet)

4 hard-boiled eggs, peeled

¼ cup finely chopped green onion

Combine the pork with the fish sauce, soy sauce, oyster sauce, salt, sugar, onion, black pepper, and browning sauce in a bowl. Cover and refrigerate for at least 30 minutes.

Place the marinated pork in a saucepan over medium-high heat. Cook, stirring, for 7 minutes, or until it is no longer pink. Add 1½ cups of water and increase the heat to high. Bring to a boil and add the eggs. Reduce the heat to medium-high, cover, and cook for 20 minutes, or until two-thirds of the water has evaporated.

Remove the saucepan from the heat. Mix in the green onion. Serve with Steamed Rice (page 61).

Catfish Pepper Stew

Cá Kho Tiêu

This is one of my family's favorite fish dishes. My husband, Chris, was not a fan of fish, but he loves this particular dish. The kho *process reduces the fishy flavor. Similar fish may be substituted for catfish.*

1½ to 2 pounds catfish, cleaned, head and tail optional

3 tablespoons fish sauce

2 tablespoons soy sauce

1 tablespoon hoisin sauce

1 tablespoon oyster sauce

½ teaspoon salt

2 tablespoons Browning Sauce (page 24), or 1 teaspoon bottled browning and seasoning sauce (such as Kitchen Bouquet)

2 tablespoons vegetable oil

¼ cup finely chopped onion plus ⅓ onion, cut into five rings

½ teaspoon black pepper

¼ cup finely chopped green onion

Cut the catfish into 1- to 2-inch pieces, and combine it with the fish sauce, soy sauce, hoisin sauce, oyster sauce, salt, browning sauce, 1 tablespoon of the oil, the chopped onion, and ¼ teaspoon of the black pepper. Cover and refrigerate for at least 1 hour. Turn occasionally.

Arrange the onion rings on the bottom of a saucepan to prevent the fish from sticking. Place the fish and its marinade on top of the onion. Cook, covered, for 5 minutes over medium heat. Add 1 cup of water and bring to a boil, then reduce the heat to medium-low. Cover and cook for 50 minutes. Reduce the heat to low and simmer for another 10 minutes, or until two-thirds of the water has evaporated (the liquid should be syrupy).

Remove the saucepan from the heat. The fish should be tender and flaky. Pour the remaining 1 tablespoon of oil, the remaining ¼ teaspoon of black pepper, and the green onion over the fish. Serve with Steamed Rice (page 61).

Tips:

If you purchase a whole catfish, the head and tail may be stewed in recipes, such as Sweet-and-Sour Catfish Soup (page 50) or Pickled Green Fish Head Soup (page 51).

A pressure cooker can be used to reduce the cooking time to 30 minutes. Be aware that the marinated sauce might not have enough time to soak into the fish, and the flavor may not be the same.

Shrimp Clay Pot

Tôm Kho   *2 servings*

Tôm kho is a simple dish served with rice and/or soup. The shrimp for kho *can range from small-size shrimp to jumbo-size prawns, but small shrimp are most common because they are one of the cheapest seafood available in Vietnam. The Vietnamese usually eat the head, tail, and shell.*

1 pound medium-size shrimp (heads are optional), deveined and butterflied (page 166)

2 teaspoons fish sauce

2 teaspoons oyster sauce

⅛ teaspoon black pepper

1 teaspoon sugar

1 tablespoon vegetable oil

1 teaspoon finely chopped garlic

¼ cup finely chopped green onion

Combine the shrimp with the fish sauce, oyster sauce, black pepper, and sugar in a medium-size bowl. Mix well, cover, and refrigerate for at least 20 minutes, then remove the shrimp from its marinade, and reserving the marinade.

Heat the oil in a frying pan or wok for 1 to 2 minutes over medium-high heat. Add the garlic and stir until golden brown. Add the shrimp and stir for 3 to 5 minutes, or until the shrimp turn pink. Pour the reserved marinade over the shrimp. If very little marinade remains, add up to ¼ cup of water. Stir for at least 2 minutes.

Remove the frying pan from the heat. Mix in the green onion. Serve with Steamed Rice (page 61).

Meat and Seafood

Meat is generally expensive in Vietnam, but the entire east coast borders the South China Sea and seafood is in abundance. Although some seafood, such as large fish, crabs, or jumbo shrimp is expensive, small fish and small shrimps are very cheap. Thus, low-income families rely on small fish, squid, field crabs, and small crustaceans instead of meat.

A regular supply of eggs makes it worthwhile to keep a productive hen. Similarly, water buffaloes and cows are more valuable as tractors in the rice fields than as food. Pigs are raised primarily for eating, thus pork is the cheapest and most common meat.

Although chicken is expensive, it is the most commonly consumed meat for special celebrations, like *Tết* (Vietnamese New Year), *Giỗ* (anniversary of the dead), or the arrival of a special guest. A good cook can produce many dishes from one chicken. Nothing goes to waste. Hearts, gizzards, livers, and other chicken organs are considered treats and are favorite Vietnamese appetizers. When I visited my relatives in Vietnam, we were feted and definitely had our share of chicken. By the time we left, we begged for fish and vegetables.

In the United States, ducks and duck eggs are more expensive than chicken and chicken eggs. The opposite is true in Vietnam where they are mostly available during the summer. In the fall, winter, and spring, farmers harvest the rice and during the summer, the rice stalks are used to feed the ducks. Frogs, dogs, cats, snakes, ants, cockroaches, and others are edible animals to Vietnamese. (I have not yet tasted dog or cat nor do I have any inclination to do so.) Dog meat is common in northern Vietnam and it is prepared in many ways, the most popular being roasting. You do not want your dog to stray in Vietnam; dog pounds do not even *exist* in Vietnam. This information is not to offend anyone but to expose the reader to the realities of Vietnamese culture. Exotic and domestic animals are eaten in Vietnam for survival, not killed for sport or amusement.

This chapter contains different ways to prepare chicken, beef, pork, seafood, and even frogs but *not* dogs, cats, snakes, ants, or cockroaches. This cookbook is intended to provide every day Vietnamese meals. Therefore, exotic meats such as dogs, cats, snakes, ants, or cockroaches are commonly served for special occasions. No dogs or cats were harmed in the making of this book.

Illustrations for preparing meat (page 165) and deveining shrimp (page 166) can be found in the appendix.

Lemongrass Chicken

Gà Xào Xã

4 servings

Soy sauce and oyster sauce give this version of gà xào xã *a very different flavor from other versions of lemongrass chicken. Any chicken parts may be used for this recipe, but wings and thighs create the juiciest and best tasting results. Traditionally in southern Vietnam, this dish is served very spicy. The Vietnamese word for hot red peppers is* ớt *and this dish is also known as* gà xào xã ớt. *Because I am not a fan of spicy food this recipe is geared toward a milder palate.*

---

2 pounds chicken, any parts
¼ cup finely chopped lemongrass
¼ cup fish sauce
¼ cup soy sauce
¼ cup rice vinegar
2 teaspoons honey
1 tablespoon oyster sauce
½ teaspoon salt
2 teaspoons minced garlic
¼ cup finely chopped onion
1 teaspoon finely chopped fresh ginger
⅛ teaspoon black pepper
¼ cup finely chopped green onion

Rinse and dry the chicken. Trim the fat but keep the skin. Chop the chicken into bite-size pieces and combine it with the lemongrass, fish sauce, soy sauce, vinegar, honey, oyster sauce, salt, garlic, onion, ginger, and black pepper in a large saucepan. Cover and refrigerate for at least 30 minutes.

In a saucepan, cook the chicken with the marinade, uncovered, for 10 minutes over high heat. Pour ½ cup of water over the chicken. Cover and reduce the heat to medium-low. Allow the chicken to simmer for 20 minutes. Remove the saucepan from the heat and stir in the green onion. Serve with Steamed Rice (page 61).

Lemon Pepper Chicken

Gà ướp Chanh Nướng

4 servings

Gà ướp chanh nướng—*chicken marinated in lemon pepper, soy sauce, garlic, and spices—is simple and inexpensive to prepare. Lemon pepper is not a traditional Vietnamese seasoning, but my aunt invented an American dish with an Asian flare. This dish will quickly become everyone's favorite party entrée.*

Make sure to use lemon pepper seasoning not lemon pepper seasoning salt, which will make the chicken very salty. Do not substitute fresh lemon and black pepper for commercially prepared lemon-pepper.

2 pounds chicken, any parts

¼ cup lemon pepper seasoning

¼ cup soy sauce

1 tablespoon honey or sugar

1 tablespoon lemon juice

2 teaspoons minced garlic

3 tablespoons butter or margarine, melted

Cut chicken breasts into bite-size pieces. Other parts may be left whole. In a bowl, combine the chicken with the lemon pepper seasoning, soy sauce, honey, lemon juice, garlic, and butter. Cover and refrigerate for at least 3 hours.

Preheat the oven to 350ºF. Line a baking pan large enough to hold the chicken in a single layer with aluminum foil.

Spread the chicken pieces in the baking pan. Pour the marinade on top. Allow the chicken to rest at room temperature for 15 minutes. Then, cover the pan with foil and bake for 30 minutes.

Remove the top sheet of foil and baste the chicken with the pan juices. Bake uncovered for 30 more minutes, or until golden brown, removing chicken wings after 20 minutes to keep them from overbaking.

Serve with Steamed Rice (page 61), bread, or salad.

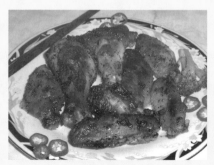

A Vietnamese Kitchen

Chicken Burgundy

Gà Nấu Riệu Vang

Chicken burgundy is a French-inspired dish. Bác Kít prepared it for the Holiday Inn's national chef contest and received second place. The chicken breasts may be substituted with other chicken parts. Red wine complements this meal well.

4 boneless skinless chicken breasts, halved

3 cubes chicken-flavor bouillon

½ teaspoon salt

1 teaspoon minced garlic

1 cup Burgundy wine

⅛ teaspoon black pepper

1 large onion, cut into 12 wedges

3 carrots, peeled and cut into 1-inch pieces

Combine the chicken with the bouillon cubes, salt, garlic, wine, and pepper in a mixing bowl. Mix well. Cover and refrigerate for at least 3 hours to overnight.

Preheat the oven to 350°F.

Remove the chicken from the marinade and place it in pan large enough to hold all the chicken. Bake for 20 minutes. Meanwhile, combine the marinade with 1 cup of water in a saucepan. Bring to a boil, then remove from the heat.

After 20 minutes, add the marinade, onion, and carrots to the chicken. Bake for 15 more minutes or until the center of the chicken is no longer pink. Serve with Steamed Rice (page 61), pasta, or bread.

Chicken Mushroom Marsala

Gà Sào Nấm

The French brought the tradition of cooking meat in wine to Vietnam during the colonial period. Dishes such as this are primarily served in French-Vietnamese restaurants, but the practice has become increasingly widespread.

Chicken mushroom marsala is one of few Vietnamese dishes without fish sauce. Even though I love fish sauce, there are others who do not enjoy it. As a chef for many years, Bác Kít found different ways to modify recipes in order to entice everyone. Henceforth, chicken mushroom marsala was created.

1 tablespoon olive oil

1 teaspoon minced garlic

2 boneless and skinless chicken breasts, cut into ½ to 1-inch strips

8 ounces fresh mushrooms, thinly sliced

1 teaspoon salt

⅛ teaspoon black pepper

¼ cup marsala

1 wedge lemon

Heat the oil in a frying pan over medium-high heat. Add the garlic. Cook, stirring, until lightly golden. Add the chicken and sauté for 5 minutes. Mix in the mushrooms, cooking for 2 more minutes. Reduce the heat to medium and add the salt and pepper. After 2 minutes, add the marsala and cook for 1 more minute or until the liquid has almost evaporated.

Remove from the heat. Squeeze the lemon over the chicken. Serve with Steamed Rice (page 61).

Roasted Cornish Hens

Gà Nướng

2 to 4 servings

The marinade in this dish can also be used for chicken, but I prefer Cornish hens because the meat is more tender and moist. I also like the feeling of accomplishment of finishing a whole hen in one meal.

---

2 (1-pound) Cornish hens

3 tablespoons soy sauce

2 tablespoons hoisin sauce

1 tablespoon finely chopped fresh ginger

2 tablespoons rice vinegar

1 tablespoon fish sauce

1 teaspoon minced garlic

⅛ teaspoon black pepper

1 teaspoon honey

Rinse the Cornish hens under cold water and drain. Remove the neck and gizzards.

Combine the soy sauce, hoisin sauce, ginger, vinegar, fish sauce, garlic, pepper, and ¼ cup water in a small bowl.

Line a roasting pan large enough to hold both Cornish hens with aluminum foil. Place the Cornish hens on the foil. Pour the soy sauce mixture on top and inside the hens. Cover the pan with more aluminum foil and refrigerate for at least 3 hours. Turn the hens to even out the flavor during the marinating time. Let the hens rest at room temperature for 20 to 30 minutes before cooking.

Preheat the oven to 350°F.

Keeping the pan covered with foil, bake for 40 minutes. Combine the honey and 1 tablespoon of water in a small bowl. Remove the pan from the oven and remove the top sheet of foil. Brush the honey mixture over the hens.

Change the oven setting from bake to broil. Broil the hens uncovered for 20 more minutes, or until golden brown. Serve with steamed rice (page 61) or a salad.

Tips: Aluminum foil helps the hens to bake evenly and to retain the marinated juices and flavors. It also makes the dishwashing process much easier.

Curried Cornish Hen

Gà Ca-ri   *2 to 4 servings*

This recipe offers another interesting way to cook and marinate poultry. The spiciness of assorted curry powders varies in intensity. Mild curry powder is not very spicy, but you may add Thai peppers or full blown spicy curry powder for a zestier flavor.

2 (1-pound) Cornish hens

¼ cup chopped onion

1 tablespoon minced garlic

2 tablespoons soy sauce

2 teaspoons mild curry powder

2 teaspoons sugar

1 teaspoon salt

½ teaspoon black pepper

½ cup vegetable oil

Rinse the Cornish hens in cold water and drain. Remove the neck and gizzards. Separate and cut the whole chicken into serving pieces. Bones may be removed if desired. Combine the chicken with the onion, garlic, soy sauce, curry, sugar, salt, and pepper. Mix well. Cover and refrigerate for at least 3 hours.

Heat the oil in a deep frying pan over medium-high heat. Separate the chicken from its marinade. Fry the chicken for 20 to 30 minutes or until golden.

Meanwhile, pour the remaining marinade to a small saucepan. Add ½ cup of water. Bring the marinade to a boil over medium-high heat. Remove from the heat.

Transfer the chicken to a serving plate. Pour the marinade over the chicken. Serve with Steamed Rice (page 61).

Beef Burgundy Stew

Bò Nấu Riệu Vang   *4 servings*

Beef burgundy stew is a French dish adopted during the colonial period. The cooking time may seem lengthy, but it is very simple to prepare. The beef becomes very tender and melts in your mouth. The marinade also works with lamb, venison, or buffalo. Red wine compliments this meal well.

2 pounds beef stew meat, cut into ½- to 1-inch cubes

6 cubes beef-flavor bouillon

¼ cup all-purpose flour

1 teaspoon salt

1 tablespoon minced garlic

1 cup Burgundy wine

1 (6-ounce) can tomato paste

⅛ teaspoon black pepper

3 slices of bacon

3 carrots, peeled and cut into 1-inch pieces

1 large onion, cut into 12 wedges

Combine the beef with bouillon cubes, flour, salt, garlic, wine, tomato paste, and pepper in a mixing bowl. Mix well. Cover and refrigerate for at least 3 hours to overnight.

Preheat the oven to 350ºF.

Fry the bacon in a large saucepan over medium-high heat for 3 to 5 minutes or until crisp. Add the beef mixture, stirring frequently for 10 minutes or until the meat is no longer pink. Pour in 3 cups of water and reduce the heat to medium. Bring to boil. Pour the beef and sauce in to a 13 x 9-inch pan. Bake for 30 minutes.

Mix the carrots and onions into the beef and bake for additional 30 minutes or until the beef is tender. Serve over Steamed Rice (page 61) or noodles.

Meat and Seafood   127

Pepper Steak
Bít Tết

Bít Tết *is beef steak, or as the French introduced it to Vietnam,* bifteck. *Since Vietnamese have a hard time saying "*bifteck,*" the name* bít tết, *pronounced "beet thet," was derived from the French term.*

2 pounds beef fillet, rib eye, or sirloin

2 tablespoons soy sauce

2 tablespoons oyster sauce

¼ cup finely chopped onion

1 tablespoon finely chopped garlic

½ teaspoon black pepper

1 tablespoon vegetable oil

Slice the beef into 3 x 4-strips. Use a tenderizer to pound several times on both sides of the strip (page 165). Combine the beef with the soy sauce, oyster sauce, onion, garlic, and black pepper in a mixing bowl. Mix well. Cover and refrigerate for at least 30 minutes. Before cooking, let the beef rest at room temperature for 10 minutes.

Heat the oil in a nonstick frying pan or wok over high heat for 2 to 3 minutes. Add the marinated beef. Sauté for 1 minute on each side, or until the desired degree of doneness is achieved. Serve with a salad, potatoes, or bread for a French meal or serve with Steamed Rice (page 61) for a Vietnamese meal.

Bồ's Favorite Burger

Thịt Burger của Bố

6 servings

Bồ is a Vietnamese word for Dad. This recipe, inspired by Bác Kít's marinated meat (page 132), was my husband Chris' idea and quickly became his favorite. You may add other ingredients such as cheese, grilled onions, or mushrooms if you wish.

1 pound ground beef
1 teaspoon fish sauce
1 teaspoon soy sauce
1 teaspoon oyster sauce
1 teaspoon hoisin sauce
¼ teaspoon salt
⅛ teaspoon black pepper

Combine the beef, fish sauce, soy sauce, oyster sauce, hoisin sauce, salt, and black pepper in a bowl. Mix well. Cover and refrigerate for at least 15 minutes. The longer the beef marinates, the more flavorful it becomes. If the beef is marinating longer than two days, freeze it.

Form the beef into 3- to 4-inch patties. Heat a nonstick frying pan over medium-high heat. Sauté the patties on both sides for 5 to 10 minutes total or until the meat is cooked to the desired degree of doneness. Transfer the burgers to a serving plate. Serve with lettuce, tomato, pickles, and/or condiments on hamburger buns.

Beef Vinegar Hot Pot

Thịt Bò Nhúng Dấm

Thịt bò nhúng dấm *is a southern Vietnamese specialty. This is a fun-filled, hands-on meal, in which everyone can participate in the preparation. Eat while you wrap!*

The longest part of this recipe is the preparation of contents of the two platters. Each serving contains fresh, thinly sliced beef and plenty of your choice of vegetables. The servings are dipped in flavorful Anchovy Sauce (page 21). If anchovy is too exotic for you, you can substitute Sweet-and-Sour Fish Sauce (page 23) or Sweet-and-Sour Hoisin Sauce (page 25).

Beef:

2 pounds fillet, beef sirloin or other lean cut of beef, thinly sliced

2 tablespoons oyster sauce

⅛ teaspoon black pepper

1 medium-size onion, sliced into thin rings

2 tablespoons finely chopped green onion

For the beef platter: Mix the beef with the oyster sauce and black pepper in a medium-size bowl. Arrange the beef on a platter. Arrange onion over the beef. Sprinkle with the green onion. Cover and refrigerate until ready to cook.

Vegetables:

1 (3-inch piece) fresh ginger

1 cucumber

1 head leaf lettuce

1 bunch mint leaves

1 bunch cilantro

½ pound bean sprouts

1 starfruit, thinly sliced (optional)

⅓ (16-ounce) package rice stick noodles (bún), cooked (page 64)

Broth:

½ cup rice vinegar

1 tablespoon finely chopped fresh ginger

2 cubes beef-flavored bouillon

1 (4-ounce) can crushed pineapple, drained

To Serve:

Anchovy Sauce (page 21), Sweet-and-Sour Fish Sauce (page 23), or Sweet-and-Sour Hoisin Sauce (page 25)

Hot water

1 (12-ounce) package rice paper (bánh tráng)

For the Vegetable Platter: Peel and slice the ginger into thin matchsticks. Peel and seed the cucumber, and slice it into thin matchsticks. Arrange the ginger, cucumber, mint, lettuce, cilantro, bean sprouts, star fruit, and noodles on a platter.

For the Broth: Combine the vinegar, ginger, bouillon cubes, pineapple, and 8 cups of water in a pot or a rice cooker. Bring to a boil over medium-low heat before serving.

To Serve: Each person starts with a large serving plate and a bowl of dipping sauce. Briefly dip the rice paper into the hot water. The hot water will instantly soften the rice paper. (Warning: Oversoaking the rice paper will make wrapping difficult.)

Lay the rice paper flat on the serving plate. Arrange a piece of lettuce in the center of the rice paper. Place a pinch of ginger, five or six bean sprouts, a pinch of noodles, a few mint leaves, three or four cilantro leaves, a few cucumber sticks, and a piece of star fruit on top of the lettuce. (Do not overload the rice paper or it will be difficult to wrap.)

Drop a few slices of marinated beef and a piece of onion into the boiling broth. Allow the beef to cook for 5 seconds, or until the desired doneness is achieved. Then place the beef and onion on top of the vegetables.

Wrap the ingredients spring roll-style (appendix, page 163). Dip the finished rolls into dipping sauce and bon appétit!

Marinated Meat

Thịt ướp

Thịt ướp *is an all-purpose marinade. It is great with pork, although it enhance the flavor of any type of meat, such as chicken, turkey, or beef.*

1 pound meat (any kind), ground or thinly sliced

1 teaspoon fish sauce

1 teaspoon soy sauce

1 teaspoon oyster sauce

1 teaspoon hoisin sauce

½ teaspoon salt

2 teaspoons finely chopped garlic

⅛ teaspoon black pepper

2 tablespoons finely chopped onion

Combine the meat, fish sauce, soy sauce, oyster sauce, hoisin sauce, salt, garlic, black pepper, and onion in a bowl. Mix well. Cover and refrigerate for at least 15 minutes. The longer the meat marinates, the more flavorful it becomes.

Crispy Meatballs

Thịt Bò Viên

Makes 20 to 25 meatballs

Thịt bò viên is a southern Vietnamese specialty. It is not your ordinary meatball. The texture is unusually crispy yet chewy. After biting into this meatball, the crispiness of the meat explodes delightfully in your mouth.

These meatballs are an excellent addition to many dishes, such as Phở (page 74), Bún Mọc (page 82), or spaghetti. The meatballs can also be served as an appetizer for dipping in Sweet-and-Sour Hoisin Sauce (page 25).

---

1 pound beef shank, stewing beef, or London broil

1 teaspoon baking powder

1 tablespoon vegetable oil

1 tablespoon fish sauce

¼ teaspoon black pepper

Remove any fat and tendons from the meat and slice the beef into ½- to 1-inch strips. In a bowl, combine the beef with the baking powder, oil, fish sauce, black pepper, and 1 tablespoon of water. Mix well. Cover and refrigerate for at least 3 hours. Process the marinated meat in a food processor until the meat is finely ground. Cover and refrigerate until ready to cook.

With clean hands, shape the meat into ½- to 1-inch balls. Bring 6 cups of water (or *phở* broth if you are serving the meatballs with *phở*) to a boil. Drop the meatballs into the broth and cook for 10 minutes, or until they float to the surface.

Tips: If you decide to marinate the meat for more than 24 hours, freeze the meat until ready to cook. You can freeze the meat for several weeks. Thaw the meatballs before processing.

When cooked in water, the cooking liquid may be saved as broth. This broth can be used instead of water for recipes, such as Glass Noodle Soup (page 81) or Tofu Eggdrop Soup (page 49).

Vietnamese Egg Loaf

Trứng Mọc

2 servings

Trứng mọc *is a steamed egg and meat dish. Ground pork is the most popular meat used, however, any ground meat will work. This tasty dish is light and healthy.*

This was one of my favorite dishes growing up, but my mom cooked trứng mọc *in an aluminum pan with very little oil or grease. I enjoyed eating it but I did not enjoy washing the pan! It was a pain to scrub. Make sure to use nonstick stainless steel or glass so you will have an easy time cleaning up afterwards.*

¼ cup chopped dried black mushrooms

½ ounce bean thread noodles (miến)

5 ounces ground pork, beef, chicken, or turkey

2 eggs, lightly beaten

⅓ cup finely chopped onion

½ teaspoon salt

1 teaspoon fish sauce

1 cup bean sprouts or shredded cabbage

⅛ teaspoon black pepper

Soak the dried mushrooms and noodles in separate bowls of hot water for 10 minutes. Drain. Cut the noodles into 1-inch lengths.

In a medium-size bowl, combine the ground meat with the mushrooms, noodles, eggs, onion, salt, fish sauce, bean sprouts, and black pepper. Knead the mixture with your hands until the all the ingredients are incorporated.

Place the meat mixture into a heatproof, nonreactive bowl. Place the bowl in the top pan of a steamer. Fill the bottom pan of the steamer with 5 cups of water. Steam over medium-high heat for 50 minutes, or until the loaf solidifies and the meat is no longer pink. Serve with Steamed Rice (page 61).

Shredded Jerky

Ruốc Bông

Makes 8 ounces

Ruốc bông *is a popular Vietnamese jerky made from pork (beef or chicken also work) stewed in fish sauce. Leftover Thanksgiving turkey is also great for* ruốc bông. *The jerky keeps in the refrigerator for several months.*

1 pound lean boneless pork
2 tablespoons fish sauce (preferably nước mắm nhĩ *quality)*
⅛ teaspoon black pepper

Thinly slice the pork with the grain so the pieces will not crumble when shredded. In a saucepan over medium-high heat, cook the pork with the fish sauce, covered, for 12 to 15 minutes, or until three-quarters of the liquid has evaporated. Stir occasionally.

Use a mortar and pestle to grind the hot meat. (It is much easier to do this while the meat is still hot.) Then, shred it into fine pieces. There are two ways to shred the meat: In a food processor using the dough blade; process for 2 minutes. Alternatively, shred the meat into fine, thin threads using clean hands. The latter option is laborious but the jerky will be fluffier and finer than when shredded with a food processor. Vietnamese prefer the fluffy and fine shredded *ruốc bông*.

Add ⅛ teaspoon black pepper to the shredded meat. Fry the shredded meat in a dry skillet over medium-low heat for 10 minutes, or until lightly golden. Serve it plain, with Steamed Rice (page 61), or bread.

Sweet-and-Sour Ribs

Sườn Chua Ngọt

Like the name suggests, sweet-and-sour ribs are slightly sweet and sour. They are definitely a treat for a special occasion.

---

2 pounds baby back pork ribs, cut into 3-inch pieces

1 tablespoon sugar

1 tablespoon soy sauce

1 tablespoon fish sauce

2 teaspoons minced garlic

¼ cup chopped onion

¼ cup rice vinegar

⅓ cup vegetable oil

1 tomato, cut into 12 wedges (optional)

Combine the ribs with the sugar, soy sauce, fish sauce, garlic, onion, and vinegar in a mixing bowl. Mix well. Cover and refrigerate for 3 hours.

Heat the oil in a frying pan or wok over medium-high heat. Remove the ribs from the marinade and sauté them for 10 to 15 minutes or until golden. Transfer to a serving plate.

Remove any remaining oil from the frying pan. Add the tomato and sauté for 1 minute over medium-high heat. Add the marinade and ½ cup of water, and bring to a boil. Remove from the heat.

Pour the tomato over the ribs. Serve with Steamed Rice (page 61).

A Vietnamese Kitchen

Sizzling Grilled Fish

Cá Nướng

Cá nướng is marinated salmon or trout roasted to perfection. This recipe may also be grilled.

2 to 3 pounds salmon or trout fillets, cut into 3-inch pieces

1 tablespoon orange zest (optional)

½ cup fresh orange juice

⅓ cup lemon juice

⅓ cup lime juice

¼ cup soy sauce

1 tablespoon honey or sugar

1 tablespoon hoisin sauce

1 teaspoon dried crushed peppers (optional)

1 tablespoon finely chopped fresh ginger

2 teaspoons minced garlic

Combine the fish with the orange zest, orange juice, lemon juice, lime juice, soy sauce, honey, hoisin sauce, dried peppers, ginger, and garlic. Mix well. Allow the fish to marinate for up to 1 hour. (If the fish is marinates longer than 1 hour, the marinade may cook the fish.)

Preheat the oven to 350°F.

Drain the marinade into a small saucepan and simmer over medium heat for 10 minutes or until it boils. Remove the saucepan from the heat and set aside.

Place the fish in a roasting pan large enough to hold all the pieces in a single layer, and bake for 30 to 40 minutes, or until the fish flakes easily. Pour the marinade over the fish. This dish is typically served with Steamed Rice (page 61), but can also be served with bread and salad.

Meat and Seafood

Tilapia with Sautéed Mushrooms
Cá Sào Ném

2 servings

Tilapia is a fresh water fish that is often found in supermarkets, but sole is a great substitute. Sole refers to a species of flatfish found in both freshwater and the ocean. This fish has lots of tiny bones, so it is best to buy it filleted.

There are many ways to prepare fish, but in my opinion, frying is the tastiest method, although it is not the healthiest. I enjoy the fragrance of roasted garlic and biting into a juicy yet crispy fish.

2 tablespoons butter

1 teaspoon minced garlic

1 (1 to 2 pounds) tilapia fillet (in 1 piece)

4 ounces fresh mushrooms, thinly sliced

1 onion, cut into 12 wedges

1 tomato, cut into 12 wedges

½ teaspoon salt

⅛ teaspoon black pepper

1 lemon wedge

Melt the butter in a frying pan over medium-high heat. Add the garlic. Cook, stirring, until golden. Dry the fish and add it to the pan. Fry both sides for 2 minutes each or until golden. Transfer the fish to a serving plate.

Add the mushrooms, onion, tomato, salt, and pepper to the remaining butter. Stir-fry for 2 more minutes or until lightly golden.

Remove from the heat. Squeeze the lemon and pour the sautéed mushroom over the fish. Serve with Steamed Rice (page 61), pasta, or bread.

A Vietnamese Kitchen

Sautéed Catfish

Cá Sốt Cà Chua

2 servings

Cá sốt cà chua is catfish sautéed with tomato, garlic, mint, and of course fish sauce. The wonderful aroma of roasted garlic and fried fish may invite the neighbors over for dinner. You may substitute other fish such as perch.

2 tablespoons fish sauce

½ teaspoon salt

½ teaspoon sugar

⅛ teaspoon black pepper

1 cup vegetable oil

1 whole catfish, (1½ to 2 pounds), cut into 2-inch fillets

3 tablespoons finely chopped onion

1 teaspoon finely chopped garlic

2 tomatoes, cut into 8 wedges each

½ cup finely chopped green onion

¼ cup finely chopped fresh cilantro

1 tablespoon rice vinegar

In a small bowl, combine 1 cup of water, the fish sauce, salt, sugar, and black pepper.

Heat the oil in a deep frying pan for 1 to 2 minutes. Fry the catfish fillets over medium-high heat until golden brown. Transfer them to a dish and blot the excess oil from the fillets with paper towels. Reserve 1 teaspoon of oil in the pan.

Heat the reserved oil over high heat. Mix in the onion and garlic, and stir until lightly golden brown. Add the tomato and stir for 2 minutes. Place the fish in the frying pan. Pour the fish sauce mixture over the fish and simmer for 10 minutes, turning occasionally.

Remove the pan from the heat. Sprinkle the green onion, cilantro, and vinegar over the fish. Serve with Steamed Rice (page 61).

Spicy Curried Frog Legs

Ếch Ca-ri ớt

4 servings

Do frogs' legs taste like chicken? The flavor is only fishy if the flesh is prepared incorrectly, but the meat is a bit chewier than chicken. This spicy marinade adds a zesty flavor to the meat, but might be too spicy for some palates.

2 pounds frogs' legs

1 cup finely chopped lemongrass

1 tablespoon minced garlic

1 tablespoon finely chopped onion

2 tablespoons soy sauce

1 tablespoon oyster sauce

½ cup white vinegar

2 tablespoons butter, melted

1 teaspoon mushroom seasoning

½ teaspoon dried red pepper flakes

½ teaspoon black pepper

½ teaspoon salt

1 teaspoon sugar

1 teaspoon curry powder

½ cups finely chopped green onion

Rinse the frogs' legs under cold water and drain. Cut each leg into 2 pieces (thigh and leg) and place them in a pot. Add the lemongrass, garlic, onion, soy sauce, oyster sauce, vinegar, butter, mushroom seasoning, pepper flakes, black pepper, salt, sugar, and curry powder to the pot. Marinate the frogs' legs at room temperature for 3 hours. If marinating longer than 3 hours, be sure to refrigerate them. Boil the frogs' legs with the marinade over medium-high heat. Cook, stirring occasionally, for 15 minutes, or until the meat is no longer pink.

Remove from the heat and add the green onion. Serve with Steamed Rice (page 61) or as an appetizer with beer.

Sautéed Shrimp

Tôm Ram

Tôm ram is yet another fun-filled, hands-on meal because the servings are wrapped like spring rolls. Everyone participates in wrapping his/her own meal.

2 pounds (medium to large) shrimp, heads and tails removed

2 teaspoons oyster sauce

2 teaspoons sesame oil

⅛ teaspoon black pepper

2 tablespoons vegetable oil

1 teaspoon finely minced garlic

¼ cup finely chopped green onion

1 (12-ounce) package rice paper (bánh tráng)

1 small head leaf lettuce, torn into bite-size pieces

⅓ (16-ounce) package rice stick noodles (bún), cooked (page 64)

1 bunch mint, stemmed

1 bunch cilantro, stemmed

¼ pound bean sprouts

½-inch piece fresh ginger, peeled and sliced

1 cup Anchovy Sauce (page 21), Sweet-and-Sour Fish Sauce (page 23), or Sweet-and-Sour Hoisin Sauce (page 25)

Hot water

Clean, shell, devein, and butterfly the shrimp (page 120). In a bowl, combine the shrimp with the oyster sauce, sesame oil, and black pepper. Mix well. Cover and refrigerate for 30 minutes.

Heat 2 tablespoons of the oil in a nonstick frying pan for 30 seconds to 1 minute over high heat. Add the garlic and stir until golden brown. Add the marinated shrimp and cook, stirring, for 2 to 3 minutes, or until the shrimp turn pink.

Remove the pan from the heat. Transfer the shrimp to a dish. Add the green onion and mix well. Arrange the lettuce, mint leaves, cilantro, bean sprouts, and noodles on a platter.

To serve, each person receives a large plate and a small bowl of dipping sauce. Briefly dip the rice paper into a bowl of hot water. The hot water will soften the rice paper instantly. (Warning: Oversoaking the rice paper will make wrapping difficult.)

Lay the rice paper flat on the serving plate. Place a piece of lettuce in the center. Place a pinch of ginger, a pinch of noodles, a few mint leaves, 3 or 4 cilantro leaves, 5 or 6 bean sprouts, and a few slices of ginger on top of lettuce. (Do not overload the rice paper or it will be difficult to wrap.) Place 2 or 3 shrimp on top of the vegetables.

Wrap the ingredients egg roll-style (appendix, page 164). Dip the finished roll into your favorite dipping sauce.

Desserts

Fruits and tea (*trà*) are the traditional Vietnamese conclusion to a meal. Desserts were not popular among until the French introduced pastries and chocolate. Nowadays, French pastries, ice cream, and yogurt are popular snacks for Vietnamese children.

Yogurt, salted prunes, and tropical fruits were my favorite snacks when I was a young girl. I can still remember the taste of the frozen vanilla yogurt lingering on my tongue, and the thought of the salty and sour prunes still makes my mouth water. I miss eating jackfruit and longan, which are fruits grown in Vietnam. Vietnamese fruits are so sweet and juicy that even a grapefruit is a delight to quench your thirst. Most exotic produce can be grown only in tropical climates. Although many Asian fruits, including jackfruit and longan, are available canned, nothing beats eating them fresh.

Cocoa is not indigenous to Vietnam. Hence, chocolate is expensive. Even as a luxury treat, chocolate is not appreciated by the average Vietnamese because of its bitter taste. (Shocking, isn't it?) However, because Vietnam produces an abundance of rice, it is this dietary mainstay that is used creatively in many desserts. Two favorites are sweet rice pudding known as *chè*, and a steamed sweet rice dish known as *xôi*. There is a main drawback of having *xôi* as a snack—a bowl of *xôi* will definitely sate your appetite; thus it is occasionally served as a meal.

Banana Coconut Pudding

Chuối Xào Dừa

Plantains are a type of starchy banana that must be cooked before being eaten. You may adjust the sugar so this dessert is as sweet as your heart desires. The gooey tapioca pearls are fun to eat and the coconut milk adds richness. Banana coconut pudding is one of my favorite desserts.

¼ teaspoon salt

2 ripe plantains, peeled and thinly sliced

¼ cup small tapioca pearls

½ cup sugar

1 (5½ ounce) can coconut milk

1 cup (4½ ounces) roasted ground peanuts

Combine 6 cups of water and ⅛ teaspoon salt in a bowl. Soak the plantains in the salt water for 15 minutes. This prevents them from turning black.

In the meantime, bring 4 cups of water to a boil in a saucepan over high heat. Add the tapioca and reduce the heat to medium-low, stirring constantly. Cook for 10 to 15 minutes or until the tapioca becomes translucent. Remove the saucepan from the heat.

Drain and rinse the bananas. Add the plantains and cook, stirring, for 10 minutes. Add sugar and remaining ⅛ teaspoon of salt and cook for 5 minutes. Stir in the coconut milk and bring to a boil. Remove the pan from the heat. The consistency of this pudding should not be too runny or too thick.

To serve, pour the pudding into a small bowls. Sprinkle ground peanuts on top.

Black Bean Pudding

Chè Đậu Đen

2 to 4 servings

Black bean pudding can be served hot or cold. Because of its light and refreshing flavor, it is often eaten as dessert or snack during the summer time in Vietnam.

1 cup dry black beans

5 cups hot water

¼ cup sugar

Rinse the beans. Soak them in hot water for at least 3 hours or overnight. In a saucepan, bring 5 cups of water to a boil over medium-high heat. Add the beans and cook for 5 minutes or until the water returns to a boil. Reduce the heat to medium-low. Allow the beans to simmer for 50 minutes or until tender, stirring occasionally. Mix in the sugar and return to a boil. Taste and adjust with additional sugar if necessary.

Black-Eyed Pea Rice Pudding

Chè Đậu Trắng

4 to 6 servings

Black-eyed pea rice pudding is complimented by coconut milk. If the pudding is too sweet for your taste, add more coconut milk. It is a great dessert or snack.

½ cup sweet rice (xôi)

1 (15-ounce) can black-eyed peas

¾ cup sugar

⅛ teaspoon salt

1 (13½-ounce) can coconut milk

Mix the sweet rice and 6 cups of water in a bowl, and soak for at least 6 hours or overnight. In another bowl, do the same with the black-eyed peas. When ready to cook, rinse the rice and the black-eyed peas. Drain for 5 to 10 minutes.

In a saucepan, combine the rice, black-eyed peas, and 4 cups of water. Cook for 30 minutes over medium heat, stirring occasionally. Add the sugar and salt, and cook, stirring, for an additional 5 minutes. Taste and adjust the sugar if necessary. Remove from the heat.

Do not shake the can of coconut milk. Skim the thicker coconut milk off the top into a small saucepan and discard the water at the bottom. Bring to a boil over medium-high heat. Remove from the heat.

To serve, pour the pudding into small bowls, and spoon 2 to 3 teaspoons of coconut milk on top.

Mung Bean Pudding

Chè Táo Sọn

4 to 6 servings

This pudding is a good complement for Mung Bean Sweet Rice (opposite page). You may adjust amount of sugar or coconut milk to your taste.

1 cup mung beans

¼ teaspoon salt

⅓ cup cornstarch

1 cup sugar

1 (13½-ounce) can coconut milk

Soak the mung beans in 3 cups of water for at least 6 hours or overnight. When ready to cook, rinse and drain the beans. Add the salt.

Line a vegetable steamer with foil. Use a fork to poke holes through the aluminum foil from inside the pan. (This will allow the steam to cook the beans evenly and prevents the beans from falling through the holes.) Place the mung beans on top of the foil.

Pour enough water into the steamer's base unit to fill it one-third full. Bring the water to a boil over high heat. Reduce the heat to medium and place the beans on top of the base. Cover and cook for 30 minutes or until tender.

In a small bowl, mix the cornstarch and ½ cup of water. In a saucepan, combine the sugar and 4 cups of water, and bring it to a boil over medium-high heat. Add the cornstarch mixture and stir constantly for 1 to 2 minutes, or until the mixture boils. Add the beans and stir until the mixture returns to the boil. Taste and adjust the sugar if necessary. Remove from the heat.

Do not shake the can of coconut milk. Skim the thicker coconut milk off the top into a small saucepan and discard the water at the bottom. Bring to a boil over medium-high heat. Remove from the heat.

To serve, pour the pudding into small bowls and spoon 2 to 3 teaspoons of coconut milk on top.

Mung Bean Sweet Rice

Xôi Đậu Xanh

Mung bean sweet rice is complemented well by Sweet Mung Bean Pudding (opposite page).

1 cup mung beans

4 cups sweet rice (xôi)

¼ teaspoon salt

1 to 2 banana leaves or aluminum foil

Soak the mung beans in 6 cups of water for at least 6 hours or overnight. In a separate bowl, soak the rice in 6 cups of water for at least 6 hours or overnight. When ready to cook, rinse the mung beans and rice. Allow both to drain for 10 minutes.

Combine the salt, beans, and rice. Line the bottom of a steamer's perforated pan with banana leaves. Use a fork to poke holes through the leaves from inside the pan. (This will allow the steam to cook the rice mixture evenly and prevents it from falling through the holes.) Place the rice mixture on top of the banana leaves.

Pour enough water into the steamer's base unit to fill it to one-third full. Bring the water to a boil over high heat. Reduce the heat to medium and place the rice mixture on top of the base. Cover and cook for 40 minutes. Remove the steamer unit from the heat.

Crumpled Sweet Rice

Xôi Vò

6 to 8 servings

Crumpled sweet rice is typically eaten for breakfast. It is my favorite sweet rice dish. This dish is also served during Tết *or* Giỗ .

2 cups (14 ounces) split mung beans

4 cups sweet rice (xôi)

¼ teaspoon salt

2 tablespoons vegetable oil

2 tablespoons sugar

1 cup shredded coconut (optional)

1 to 2 banana leaves or aluminum foil

In a bowl, soak the mung beans with 6 cups of water. In a separate bowl, soak the sweet rice in 6 cups of water. Soak the beans and rice for at least 6 hours, or overnight. When ready to cook, rinse the mung beans and sweet rice. Allow both to drain for 10 minutes.

Mix the mung beans with ⅛ teaspoon of the salt. Line the bottom of a steamer's perforated pan with banana leaves. Use a fork to poke holes through the leaves from inside the pan. (This will allow the steam to cook the rice mixture evenly and prevents it from falling through the holes.) Place the mung beans on top of the foil or banana leaves.

Pour enough water into the steamer's base unit to fill it one-third full. Bring the water to a boil over high heat. Reduce the heat to medium and place the mung beans on top of the base. Cover and cook for 30 minutes. Leaving the banana leaves in the top pan, transfer the mung beans to a bowl. Mash the hot beans with a large wooden spoon. (It is much easier to mash the beans while hot.)

Stir two-thirds of the beans and ⅛ teaspoon of salt to the rice. Transfer the rice mixture into the same steamer's top pan. Cover and cook for 40 minutes, or until the rice is soft and moist. Remove the steamer from the heat. Add the remaining mung beans, the vegetable oil, and the sugar to the rice mixture. Stir in the coconut, if desired. Taste the rice and adjust with additional sugar if necessary. Serve as is, or with Mung Bean Pudding (page 148).

A Vietnamese Kitchen

Gấc Sweet Rice

Xôi Gấc   6 to 8 servings

Xôi Gấc is a dessert or a breakfast dish. It is often served during festive celebrations, such as Tết. Gấc (Momordica cochinensis) is a fruit indigenous to Vietnam. It is the size of a medium cantaloupe, with a spiny orange or red shell. The pulp and seeds are used primarily to enhance the color and subtle nutty flavor of this dish. It is not easily found in America, hence my aunt substituted tomato paste and red food coloring.

---

1 fresh gấc or ¼ cup tomato paste

4 cups sweet rice (xôi)

½ teaspoon red food coloring

¼ teaspoon salt

1 tablespoon white wine (if using gấc)

1 to 2 banana leaves or aluminum foil

¼ cup sugar

2 teaspoons vegetable oil

1 cup shredded coconut (optional)

If using fresh *gấc*, cut it in half. Scoop the pulp and seeds into a bowl. Add the wine and soak overnight, covered, in the refrigerator. (The wine intensifies the crimson color of *gấc*.) In another bowl, mix the sweet rice with 5 cups of water, the red food coloring, and the salt. Soak for at least 6 hours, or overnight. When ready to cook, rinse the rice and drain it for 10 minutes.

Mix the *gấc* mixture or tomato paste into the rice. Line the bottom of a steamer's perforated pan with banana leaves. Use a fork to poke holes through the leaves from inside the pan. (This will allow the steam to cook the rice mixture evenly and prevents it from falling through the holes.) Place the rice mixture on top of the foil or banana leaves.

Pour enough water into the steamer's base unit to fill it one-third full. Bring the water to a boil over high heat. Reduce the heat to medium and place the rice on top of the base. Cover and cook for 40 minutes. Remove the steamer unit from the heat.

Add the sugar and vegetable oil to the rice. Mix well. Cover and cook for an additional 10 minutes, or until the rice is soft and moist.

Remove the steamer unit from the heat. Taste the rice and adjust with additional sugar if necessary. Stir in the coconut.

Vietnamese Gelatin

Thạch   *Makes 16 ounces or 2 to 4 servings*

This homemade Vietnamese gelatin is very similar to Jell-O brand gelatin. However, the texture is firmer and it will set at room temperature after about an hour.

Using Vietnamese gelatin, you can also create a refreshing dessert drink (opposite page). This is the basic recipe for vanilla-flavored gelatin, but you may add fruits such as bananas or strawberries to the recipe. Do not add acidic fruit, such as oranges, pineapple, or kiwis as they will break down the gelling agent in the agar-agar and your gelatin will be runny.

*2 teaspoons agar-agar
    powder*

2 tablespoons sugar

½ teaspoon vanilla

*¼ teaspoon red food
    coloring*

2 cups hot water

*1 banana or 4 strawberries,
    thinly sliced (optional)*

Combine the agar-agar powder, sugar, vanilla, red coloring, and hot water. Stir until all the ingredients are dissolved. Mix in the fruits. Pour into a 4-cup container and allow to set at room temperature for 1 hour.

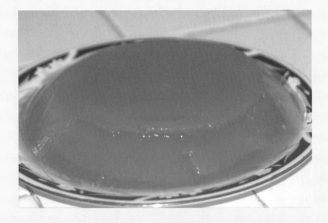

Gelatin Drink

Nước Thạch Đường

This Vietnamese gelatin is great for Saigon's hot and humid summer climate. This icy cold drink makes a very refreshing dessert.

---

2 *tablespoons sugar*

4 *ounces Vietnamese gelatin (opposite page), thinly sliced into long strips*

Combine 1½ cups of water and the sugar in a tall glass. Stir until the sugar dissolves. Add the gelatin. Mix well. Adjust the sweetness to your liking. Add a few ice cubes for a colder drink.

Vietnamese Vanilla Yogurt
Da Ua

Makes 18 to 20 (4-ounce) jars

Along with ice cream, Vietnamese-style yogurt is a favorite snack. It is creamier and more sour than American yogurt and may be eaten chilled or frozen. This recipe is for vanilla-flavored yogurt, but chocolate, or strawberries, cherries, or other fruits may be added—experiment to see which you prefer. Da ua was one of my favorite snacks when I was growing up in Vietnam.

The fermenting time is at least 6 hours. Start the yogurt process early in the morning if you would like to have it ready by dinnertime. Please read this recipe thoroughly before starting. For successful yogurt, it is very important to follow the steps exactly. Gather all of the ingredients and tools before you begin to cook.

½ gallon low-fat or whole milk

1 (14-ounce) can sweetened condensed milk

½ cup sugar

1 cup (8 ounces) plain yogurt (regular or fat-free)

18 to 20 (4-ounce) lidded jars (baby-food jars are good for this)

Fill a large saucepan with 2½ quarts of water. Heat the water for 6 to 7 minutes over medium-high heat, or until the temperature reaches 160°F. Use a cooking thermometer to gauge this; the temperature must be accurate.

While the water is heating, combine the milk, condensed milk, and sugar in a second large saucepan. Stir continuously—the direction you stir does not matter, but it is important to be consistent. Always stir in the same direction. Cook the mixture for 4 to 5 minutes, or the temperature reaches 110°F. Again, use a cooking thermometer. Remove the saucepan from the heat. Add the yogurt and keep stirring until it dissolves into the mixture.

Pour the yogurt mixture into each jar, filling them to the brim, and seal each with a lid. Rinse the saucepan that had been used to heat the milk mixture. Place half the jars in this saucepan, and half into a third saucepan. Pour the hot water into each pan, keeping the water level below the necks of the jars. Cover each saucepan tightly with plastic wrap, then place its lid firmly

on top of the plastic wrap. Wrap the saucepans in 2 blankets, and place in a warm room. Add more blankets on top and allow the mixture to set for 6 hours. Then, unwrap the pans and remove the jars. Refrigerate the yogurt overnight, or until the it solidifies. Keep refrigerated, or freeze.

Tips: If the warm yogurt sets for longer than 6 hours, it will become more sour. Adjust the time to your liking. Yogurt keeps for 2 weeks refrigerated, or a month if frozen.

Meal Planning

If Vietnamese food is unfamiliar to you, bookmark this chapter, which supplies helpful suggestions for creating both everyday meals and dinners for special celebrations. Vietnamese cuisine is very flexible. Most of the recipes in this cookbook are basic guidelines, not rigid formulas. The recipes will still taste good if the ingredients are altered or omitted. The dishes are also easily modified to become vegetarian or vegan, or milder or spicier. Everyone's tastes are different. Modify the recipes to your liking.

Veggie Meals

The following four menus are examples of meat dishes modified to vegetarian dishes.

Most nonmeat recipes in this cookbook include fish sauce or oyster sauce. Sometimes, soy sauce is a good replacement for fish sauce. However, some other dishes may not be as appetizing made without these seasonings.

Spinach and Tofu Delight (Vegan)
Vietnamese Spinach Stir-Fry (page 100)
Sautéed Tofu (replace the fish sauce with soy sauce) (page 103)
Steamed Rice (page 61)

Sweet-and-Sour Vegetarian Meal (Vegan)
Pickled Mustard Greens (page 26)
Sautéed Zucchini (page 109)
Steamed Rice (page 61)

Fried Rice Galore (Vegetarian)
Egg Fried Rice or Veggie Fried Rice (page 65 or 68)
Salad with Lemon Dessing (page 53)
Yogurt (page 154)

Tofu Delight (Vegetarian)
Tofu Egg Drop Soup (page 49)
Vietnamese Spinach Stir-Fry (page 100)
Sautéed Tofu or Egg Sautéed Tofu (page 103 or 104)
Steamed Rice (page 61)

Traditional Meals

Anyone can create many great combinations from this cookbook. A simple meal consists of steamed rice, soup, a vegetable dish, and/or a meat dish. The noodle and fried rice dishes may be used as stand alone meals. The following eight meal-planning guidelines are examples of everyday meals.

Soup and Stew Meal
Bok Choy Soup (page 43)
Crispy Stir-Fried Bean Sprouts (page 91)
Egg and Pork Stew (page 115)
Steamed Rice (page 61)

Catfish Meal
Catfish Pepper Stew (page 116)
Sweet-and-Sour Catfish Soup (use the fish head
and tail from the stew) (page 50)
Steamed Rice (page 61)

Phở Delight
Salad with Lemon Dressing (page 53)
Vietnamese Beef Noodle Soup (*Phở*) (page 74)

Zesty Soup Meal
Salad with Lemon Dressing (page 53)
Huế-Style Beef Noodle Soup (page 76)

Meaty Greens Meal
Stuffed Squash Soup (page 47)
Stir-fried Green Beans (page 97)
Roasted Cinnamon Patty (page 36)
Steamed Rice (page 61)

A Vietnamese Kitchen

Chowder Meal
Eggplant Chowder (page 44)
Sizzling Stir-Fried Bok Choy (page 94)
Meat Omelets (page 37)
Steamed Rice (page 61)

Simple and Light Meal
Vietnamese Chicken Coleslaw (page 55)
Chicken and Rice Soup (page 69)

Country-Style Meal
Pickled Mustard Greens (page 26)
Tofu Egg Drop Soup (page 49)
Shrimp Clay Pot (page 118)
Steamed Rice (page 61)

Special Occasion Meals

These meals are prepared primarily on special occasions such as weddings, Giỗ, and Tết.

Crab Soup Mumbo Jumbo
Asparagus Crab Soup (page 52)
Banana-Leaf Meatloaf (page 35)
Egg Rolls (page 32)

Hands On Meal
The preparation for this meal is more time consuming than the cooking, but it is a fun hand on meal. Every one wraps his or her own food.

Asparagus Crab Soup (page 52)
Beef Vinegar Hot Pot (page 130)

Hands On Seafood Meal
Egg Drop Soup (page 48)
Sautéed Shrimp (page 141)

Giỗ Feast
This meal is commonly served during Giỗ, the anniversary of the dead. Boiled chicken is often included.

Crumpled Sweet Rice (page 150)
Mung Bean Pudding (page 148)
Vietnamese Chicken Coleslaw (page 55)
Glass Noodle Soup (page 81)

Grilled Pork Meal
Rice Grilled Pork (page 78)
Egg Rolls (page 32)

A Vietnamese Kitchen

Appendix

Spring Roll Assembly

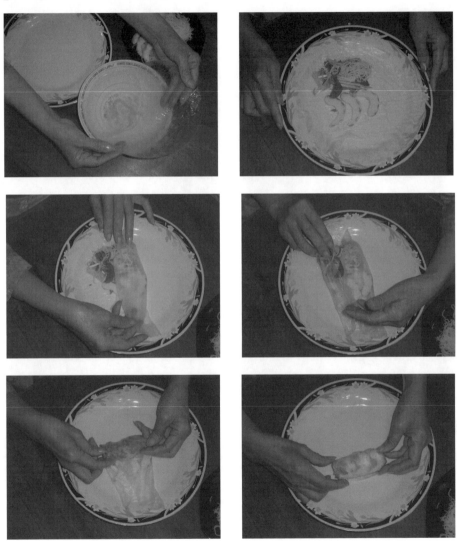

Egg Roll Assembly

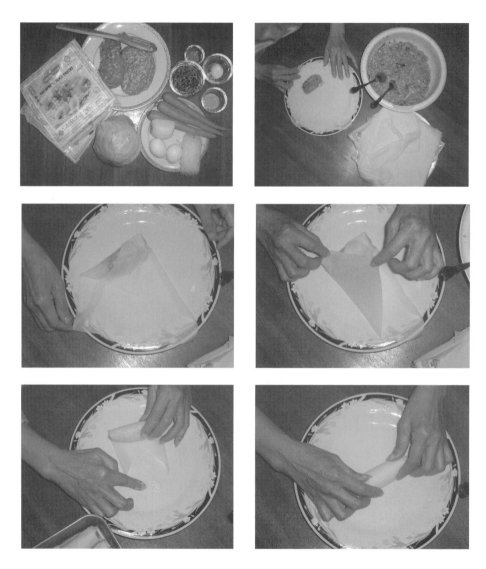

Preparing Meat

Slice the meat perpendicular to the grain.

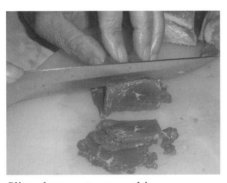 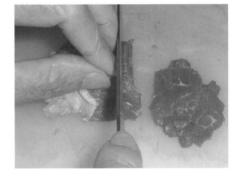

Slice the meat paper thin.

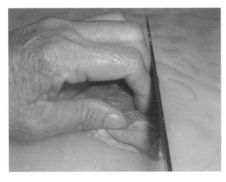

Make sure to align your fingernails against the knife when slicing. This will prevent accidental slicing of fingers.

Deveining Shrimp

Clean the shrimp by removing the head and the shell.

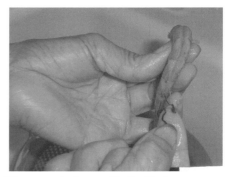

Score the shrimp with a sharp knife as illustrated above. Pull off the thin dark vein with your fingers.

Glossary

Agar-agar powder — Also known by its Japanese name, *kanten*. Agar is derived from Gracilaria (*Gleidium purpuras-cens*), bright red algae. Agar gels at approximately 88°F, but once formed does not melt below 136°F. Agar is an excellent gelling agent and thickener, used in many processed foods such as doughnuts, marmalade, jelly candy, cheese and puddings.

Anchovy sauce (*mắm nêm*) — An anchovy paste used for dipping sauces. It is less pungent than shrimp paste.

Anise — A plant, native to the Mediterranean region, with clusters of small pale yellow flowers and licorice-flavored seeds. Aniseed is used as to flavor Vietnamese soups.

Áo dài — A Vietnamese traditional dress for women and men. The direct translation for *áo dài* is "long shirt."

Bánh tráng — See rice paper.

Bean sprouts (*giá*) — Sprouted seeds, such as mung or soybean. Bean sprouts are available from Asian grocery stores and may also be found in the produce section of American supermarkets.

Bok choy —This distinctive vegetable, with white stems and dark green leaves, is a type of cabbage available in most supermarkets. It is also known as white Chinese cabbage. There is also Shanghai or baby bok choy, a smaller version of the same vegetable. Bok choy is used in soups and stir-fries. Rinse thoroughly before using.

Bouillon cubes — Packaged seasoned cubes used to make broth. The cubes are added to soups as well as to stir-fried dishes. Some bouillon cubes contain MSG, but there are also brands that do not; please read the label carefully if you need to avoid MSG. Here are a few bouillon cubes mentioned in this cookbook:
Bún bò Huế— contain sugar, salt, MSG, and spices used especially for *Bún bò Huế* soup (page 76).

167

Phở — beef, chicken, or vegetable cubes used for *phở* soup (page 74). These cubes also contain aniseed.

Chicken-flavored bouillon cubes.

Beef-flavored bouillon cubes.

Bún bò Huế and *phở* cubes are available in many Asian grocery stores. Chicken- and beef-flavored bouillon cubes are available in most American supermarkets.

Chinese mustard greens or mustard greens — A leafy green vegetable that Vietnamese cooks like to pickle or use in soups or stir-fries. If you find the pickled mustard greens too pungent, blanch them in cold water.

Cilantro — See mints and herbs.

Curry powder (*Cà-ri Bơ*) — A spice blend available in mild and spicy. The typical ingredients are garlic, turmeric, onion, and pepper. This curry is available in Asian supermarkets.

Dầu hào — See oyster sauce.

Dưa chua — A Vietnamese term for pickled Chinese mustard greens.

Egg roll wrappers — Thin sheets of square, triangular or circular dough primarily composed of flour, water, and eggs used for egg rolls.

Fish sauce (*nước mắm*) — An extract of anchovies, water, wine, and salt. It is very salty.

Gấc (*Momordica cochinensis*) — An orange or red fruit indigenous to Vietnam. It is the size of a medium cantaloupe, with a spiny shell. *Gấc* is primarily used to enhance the color and subtle nutty flavor of a sweet rice dish called *Xôi gấc* (page 151).

Gía — See bean sprouts.

Gia vị bò kho — A beef stew spice containing powdered chili, paprika, garlic, onion, star anise, cinnamon, and fennel cloves.

Gia vị bún bò huế — An spice blend containing powdered chili, paprika, ginger, and onion.

Gia vị nấu phở — A spice blend for *phở* packed in a tea bag, containing ground anise, cloves, cinnamon, allspice, salt, and ginger.

Ginger — A knobby root with a pungent and spicy flavor. Asian cooks prefer fresh ginger for sauces and/or stir-fries. Ginger is also believed to have medicinal properties and is sometimes used to soothe upset stomachs and boost energy.

Giỗ — A Vietnamese holiday celebrating the anniversary of the dead.

Hoisin sauce (*tương ăn phở*) — Also known as plum sauce. It is a dark, sweet-and-sour sauce commonly used in Chinese cuisine for Peking duck and moo-shu pork. It is great as a dip as well as for stir-fries.

Hot chili sauce (*tương ớt*) — A spicy chili sauce used to accent many dishes. Tương ớt Sriracha, made from sun-ripened chiles is the most common brand.

Húng phở — See mints and herbs.

Lemongrass (*xả*) — A grass that grows in tropical climates, but may also be cultivated in American herb gardens. Very pungent herb and normally used in small amounts, the light lemon flavor of this grass blends well with garlic, chilies, and cilantro. This herb is frequently used in curries as well as in seafood soups. The entire stalk of grass is used and the bulb is bruised and minced.

MSG (monosodium glutamate)—A white crystalline chemical compound with a meatlike flavor. In American supermarkets, it sold under the brand name Ac'cent. MSG is often used in Asian cooking.

Mints and Herbs — Like rice, many different kinds of herbs and mints are used in Vietnamese cooking. Each type has a different flavor and purpose. Here are a few of the most popular:

Cilantro (ngò) — A common herb used for garnishes and flavoring. It is usually described as warm, nutty, and spicy. Also known as Chinese parsley, this herb is found in American supermarkets. It resembles Western flat-leaf parsley.

 Húng phở — Also known as Thai basil. Used for *phở*, this herb has an anise-like flavor with a hint of cloves.

Rau ôm — This citrus-scented herb, known as rice paddy herb, has a hint of lemony flavor. It enhances Vietnamese spinach dishes (page 100) and fish soups.

Rau răm — This herb, also known as Vietnamese coriander or polygonum, has a coriander-like scent and a lemony flavor. It has a pink stem and purplish leaves. *Rau răm* is a great addition to soups. (Mix regular mint and cilantro if you can't find *rau răm* at Asian groceries.)

 *Tía tô* — A purple-leafed mint, known as red perilla. This herb has a cinnamon and anise fragrance that compliments Eggplant Chowder (page 44).

Mắm nêm — See anchovy sauce.

Mắm tôm — See shrimp paste.

Mắm tương — See soy sauce.

Mung beans — Round beans with a green skin. They are used whole or, more commonly, split and hulled. Split and hulled mung beans are small and yellow. These are also often sprouted, and mung bean sprouts are found in most Asian grocery stores.

Mushrooms, dried black (nấm mèo hay nhĩ) — Large dried black mushrooms, also known as tree-ear or cloud-ear fungus or dried *kikurage* (their Japanese name). These mushrooms are available in Asian grocery stores. They must be softened before use by soaking them in hot water for at least 15 minutes.

Mushroom seasoning — A substitute for MSG, containing powdered dried mushrooms, mushroom extract, salt, and vegetable extract. This seasoning enhances the flavor of many Vietnamese dishes, however, it is optional because of its limited availability. It is sold primarily in Asian communities.

Straw mushrooms — These mushrooms are sold canned, dried, and fresh in produce sections that carry multiple varieties of mushrooms. They are usually available in Asian markets.

Mustard Greens — See Chinese mustard greens

Nấm mèo — See mushrooms, dried black.

Noodles —There are many varieties of noodles. Here are a few types used in this cookbook:

Rice sticks or *vermicelli* (*bún*) — Thin, white dried noodles made from rice, available dried or fresh. The dried form is more widely available in the US than fresh noodles. Look for them in the Asian section of supermarkets or health food stores, or in the noodle section of Asian groceries. Rice sticks are served in soups such as *Bún Riêu* (see page 84) or with barbecued meat such as *Bún Thịt Nướng* (see page 80).

Bean thread or *glass noodles* (*miến*) — Very thin, dried noodles that are translucent, and elastic when cooked. They are made from mung beans and cassava, and come in small (2- to 8-ounces) bunches. They need to be soaked in warm water for at least 10 to 15 minutes before cooking. Bean thread noodles are available at Asian groceries, health food stores, and some American supermarkets.

Asian phở noodles (*bánh phở*) — Medium-wide, white rice noodles commonly used for *phở* (see page 74 or 72). These noodles can be bought dried or fresh in Asian markets. Dried noodles more widely available.

Egg noodles (*mì*) — Wheat-based noodles made with eggs, available dried or fresh. Dried noodles more widely available, and may be found in some American supermarkets. Egg noodles make for a great vegetable stir-fry or a yummy steaming soup.

Bún bò Huế noodles — A thicker version of rice noodles used mainly for *Bún Bò Huế* (see page 76). Often found in Asian supermarkets.

Nước mắm — See fish sauce.

Oyster sauce (*dầu hào*) — An oyster-extract, used for marinating meat. Oyster sauce helps tenderize meat and flavor dishes.

Rau ôm — See mints and herbs.

Rau răm — See mints and herbs.

Rice (*gạo*) —There are many types of rice. This cookbook describes cooking methods for long-grain white rice and broken rice. Rice is such a staple that you'll find at least 25 to even 50 pounds of rice in every Vietnamese household at all times. One of my favorite rice brands is Buddha. You may find these types of rice at American supermarkets; you may also find jasmine rice at health food stores, gourmet markets, and Asian supermarkets. If you are interested in learning more about rice, please refer to www.ricecafe.com.

Here are a few kinds of rice used in this book:

White or *Brown Rice* (*gạo*) — Regular long-grain rice. White rice is served for most meals.

Jasmine Rice (*gạo thơm*) — Sweet-smelling long-grain rice with an aroma similar to popcorn, when cooked. The texture of jasmine rice is more tender and stickier than that of regular white rice.

Broken rice (*gạo tấm*) — Regular long-grain rice broken and processed into small pieces. It has a dryer texture than long-grain rice. Restaurants and food vendors serve steamed broken rice (cơm tấm) with marinated meat and seafood.

Sweet or *Sticky Rice* (*gạo nếp*) — Short-grain glutinous rice with a white, opaque kernel. *Xôi* is often steamed with different foods, such as mung beans, shredded coconut, peanuts, or meat and is usually served at breakfast.

Rice paper, dried (*bánh tráng*) — A square or round of paper-

thin dough made of rice, flour, salt, and water. Rice paper is used to wrap egg rolls (page 32), spring rolls (page 31), and *Thịt Bò Nhúng Dấm* (page 130). It is very brittle and may be difficult to wrap. It is available at most Asian supermarkets.

A Vietnamese Kitchen

Shrimp paste (*mắm tôm*) — Fermented shrimp. Considered a delicacy, shrimp paste is an acquired taste; its unpleasant aroma may drive away people who are unfamiliar with it.

Soy sauce — Sauce made from fermented soybeans. Golden Mountain is one of my favorite brands.

Star fruit — Also known as carambola. Star fruit is a waxy, golden-yellow to green fruit, that has a five-pointed star shape when sliced widthwise. It can be sour or sweet. Star fruit is used in sweet-and-sour soups, such as *Canh Chua* (see page 50).

Tamarind soup base mix — Powdered tamarind with sugar and salt, used as a souring agent for such soups as *Canh Chua* (see page 50). It is available at Asian groceries.

Tara stem (*Alocasia odora*)— A type of elephant ear known as *Bạc Hà*. It has a crispy texture and lemony flavor which goes well in sweet-and-sour soups, such as *Canh Chua* (see page 50). Tara stem is primarily available in Asian markets.

Tết — Vietnamese New Year's celebration. The Vietnamese follow the Chinese lunar calendar, based on the cycles of the moon. The beginning of the year can fall anywhere between late January and the middle of February because of this cyclical dating method.

Tía tô — See mints and herbs

Tofu (*Đậu Hủ*) — Also known as soybean curd, a soft, cheeselike product made by curdling fresh hot soymilk and pressing the curds into a solid block.

Tương ăn phở — See hoisen sauce.

Vietnamese spinach — Also known as *ung choy* or water spinach. It is very popular and easily grown in Vietnam. Vietnamese spinach is used for stir-fried dishes. It is available in many Asian markets.

References

Bladhalm, Linda. *The Asian Grocery Store Demystified*. Los Angeles: Renaissance Books, 1999.

Choi, Trieu Thi and Isaak, Marcel. *The Foods of Vietnam*. Singapore: Periplus Editions, 1997.

Clark, Pamela, ed. *Easy Vietnamese-Style Cookery*. Sydney: Australian Women's Weekly Home Library, 1995.

D'Aprix, David. *The Fearless International Foodie Conquers Pan-Asian Cuisine*. New York: Random House, 2001.

Lau, Anita Loh-Yien. *Asian Greens*. New York: St. Martin's Griffin, 2001.

Ngo, Bach and Gloria Zimmerman. *The Classic Cuisine of Vietnam*. New York: Barron's/Woodbury, 1979.

Nguyen-Dinh-Hoa. *Vietnamese-English Dictionary*. Ruthland, Vermont: Charles E. Tuttle Company, 1966.

Nguyen, Van Khon. *English-Vietnamese / Vietnamese-English Dictionary*. California: Dainam Publishing Co., 1987.

Routhier, Nicole. *The Foods of Vietnam*. New York: Stewart, Tabori & Chang, 1989.

Index

A Vietnamese Kitchen

Vietnamese Interest Titles from Hippocrene Books ...

Beginner's Vietnamese
517 PAGES • 0-7818-0411-6 • $19.95PB • (253)

Vietnamese-English/English-Vietnamese Standard Dictionary
12,000 ENTRIES • 501 PAGES • 0-87052-924-2 • $19.95PB • (529)

Vietnamese-English/English-Vietnamese Dictionary & Phrasebook
517 PAGES • 0-7818-0991-6 • $24.95PB • (104)

From Hippocrene's Asian Cookbook Library ...

Afghan Food & Cookery
Helen Saberi

This classic source for Afghan cookery is now available in an updated and expanded North American edition! This hearty cuisine is based on such staples as lamb, flatbreads, rice pilafs, chickpeas, spinach, and yogurt, all flavored with delicate spices. The author's informative introduction describes traditional Afghan holidays, festivals, and celebrations; she also includes a section on "The Afghan Kitchen," which provides essentials about cooking utensils, spices, basic ingredients, and methods.
312 PAGES • ILLUSTRATIONS • 0-7818-0807-3 • $14.95PB • (510)

The Art of Uzbek Cooking
Lynn Visson

An historical crossroads in Central Asia, Uzbekistan and its cuisine reflect the range of nationalities that formed the country and continue to flourish there. This collection of 175 authentic Uzbek recipes includes chapters on Appetizers & Salads, Soups, Meat, Poultry & Fish, Stuffed Pastries, Dumplings, and more.
278 PAGES • ILLUSTRATIONS • 0-7818-0669-0 • $24.95HC • (767)

The Best of Regional Thai Cuisine
Chat Mingkwan

Thai people have taken the best of culinary influences from nearby countries such as China, India, Cambodia, Indonesia, Laos, Malaysia, Burma and Vietnam, and adapted them to produce distinctly Thai creations like Galangal Chicken, Green Curry Chicken, and Three Flavor Prawns.

In addition to more than 150 recipes, all adapted for the North American kitchen, Chef Mingkwan provides helpful sections on Thai spices and ingredients as well as cooking techniques.
216 PAGES • 0-7818-0880-4 • $24.95HC • (26)

The Best of Taiwanese Cuisine
Karen Hulene Bartell

Dishes from the four corners of China are found in Taiwanese kitchens and restaurants: noodles, dumplings and Mongolian Lamb Barbecue from northern China; sauces and herbs from the east are featured in recipes like Piquant Lime Chicken in Swallow's Nest; hot and spicy foods from the Szechuan region; and delicately seasoned seafood from southern China. More than a collection of 100 delicious Taiwanese recipes, this cookbook is divided into seasons and traditional celebrations such as Lunar New Year, Dragon Boat Festival, Chinese Valentine's Day, and Mid-Autumn Moon—with a complete menu for each one.
122 PAGES • B/W PHOTOS/DRAWINGS • 0-7818-0855-3 • $24.95HC • (46)

Exotic Tastes of Sri Lanka
Suharshini Seneviratne

This unique cookbook highlights the range of flavors of Sri Lankan cuisine, which has been influenced by its proximity to India, as well as successive Portuguese, Dutch, and British occupations. Staple ingredients include rice, coconut, and aromatic herbs and spices such as curry leaves, mint, coriander, and fennel seeds. Sample menus, explanations of spice uses and availability, typical cooking techniques, and descriptions of traditional utensils complement the 157 traditional recipes.
228 PAGES • 0-7818-0966-5 • $24.95HC • (538)

Flavorful India
Treasured Recipes from a Gujarati Family
Priti Chitnis Gress

This collection of authentic family recipes will introduce you to some of India's most flavorful, yet often overlooked, culinary offerings. The simple, delectable recipes are written for the home cook and adapted to the North American kitchen. An introduction to Gujarati culture, sections on spices, ingredients, and utensils, and charming line drawings bring the flavors of India to life.

147 PAGES • ILLUSTRATIONS • 0-7818-1060-4 • $22.50HC • (92)

Healthy South Indian Cooking
Alamelu Vairavan and Patricia Marquardt

With an emphasis on the famed Chettinad cooking tradition of southern India, these 197 mainly vegetarian recipes will allow home cooks to create exotic fare like Masala Dosa with Coconut Chutney, Pearl Onion and Tomato Sambhar, Chickpea and Bell Pepper Poriyal, and Eggplant Masala Curry. These easy-to-prepare dishes are exceptionally delicious and nutritious, featuring wholesome vegetables and legumes flavored with delicate spices. Each of these recipes includes complete nutritional analysis. Also included are sample menus of complementary dishes and innovative suggestions for integrating South Indian dishes into traditional Western meals. A section on the varieties and methods of preparation for dals, a multilingual glossary of spices and ingredients, and sixteen pages of color photographs make this book and clear and concise introduction to the healthy, delicious cooking of southern India.

348 PAGES • COLOR PHOTOS • 0-7818-0867-7 • $24.95HC • (69)

Imperial Mongolian Cooking
Recipes from the Kingdoms of Genghis Khan
Marc Cramer

Imperial Mongolian Cooking is the first book to explore the ancient culinary traditions of Genghis Khan's empire, opening a window onto a fascinating culture and a diverse culinary tradition virtually unknown in the West.

These 120 easy-to-follow recipes encompass a range of dishes, including Bean and Meatball Soup, Spicy Steamed Chicken Dumplings, Turkish Swordfish Kabobs, and Uzbek Walnut Fritters. The recipes are from the four *khanates* (kingdoms) of the empire that includes modern-day Mongolia, Chinese-controlled Inner Mongolia, China, Bhutan, Tibet, Azerbaijan, Kyrgystan, Tajikistan, Turkmenistan, Uzbekistan, Kazakhstan, Georgia, Armenia, Syria, and Turkey. The author's insightful introduction, a glossary of spices and ingredients, and sample menus will assist the home chef in creating meals fit for an emperor!

211 PAGES • 0-7818-0827-8 • $24.95HC • (20)

The Indian Spice Kitchen
Monisha Bharadwaj

This richly produced, wonderfully readable cookbook, written by the food consultant to the celebrated London restaurant, Bombay Brasserie, takes you on an unforgettable journey along the spice routes of India with more than 200 authentic recipes and stunning color photographs throughout. Simple step-by-step recipes, all adapted for the North American kitchen, allow the home chef to create delicious dishes with precious saffron, delicately fragrant turmeric, mustard seeds, and chilies.

The recipes are arranged by featured ingredient in a full range of soups, breads, vegetarian and meat dishes, beverages, and desserts. Among those included are Lamb with Apricots, Cauliflower in Coconut and Pepper Sauce, and Nine Jewels Vegetable Curry. This cookbook includes historical and cultural information on each ingredient, facts on storage and preparation, medicinal and ritual uses, and cooking times and serving suggestions for each recipe.

240 PAGES • COLOR PHOTOS • 0-7818-0801-4 • $17.50PB • (513)

Japanese Home Cooking
Hans Kizawa and Rina Goto-Nance

Husband and wife team Hans and Rina have assembled this unique collection of recipes for Japanese "comfort foods" and everyday meals. Among these 100 recipes are all varieties of sushi and miso soups, along with other specialties like Sukiyaki, Cold Somen with Ham and Veggies, Tofu Steak with Mushroom, and Squid and Daikon. Photographs illustrate techniques and information on equipment, basic ingredients, and Japanese pronunciation ensure that even novice cooks can produce spectacular results. Full of anecdotes and observations, this book is a delightful addition to any kitchen.
160 PAGES • 0-7818-0881-2 • $24.95HC • (27)

Simple Laotian Cooking
Penn Hongthong

This cookbook offers 172 recipes, including a section on the traditional *Lob*, a dish usually made with beef and served with sticky rice and vegetables. A glossary defines staple ingredients like bamboo shoots, cilantro, coconut milk, ginger, kaffir lime leaves, and lemongrass. The author also incorporates Western ingredients, making Laotian cuisine easy to master.
225 PAGES • 0-7818-0963-0 • $24.95HC • (522)